Dead Letter Perfect
in association with Par[k]
present

The Gathered Leaves

Andrew Keatley

The Gathered Leaves premiered at Park Theatre, London,
on 15 July 2015

The Gathered Leaves

Andrew Keatley

Cast

Olivia Pennington	Jane Asher
Emily Pennington	Georgina Beedle
William Pennington	Clive Francis
Giles Pennington	Alexander Hanson
Simon Pennington	Tom Hanson
Aurelia Ndjeya	Amber James
Samuel Pennington	Nick Sampson
Alice Pennington	Katie Scarfe
Sophie Pennington	Anna Wilson-Jones
Young Giles Pennington	Hamish Brewster
Young Samuel Pennington	Oliver Buckner

Creative Team

Director	Antony Eden
Casting Director	Ellie Collyer-Bristow
Designer	James Perkins
Lighting Designer	Paul Colwell
Associate Lighting Designer	Stella Cheung
Production Manager	Gareth Sowerby
Stage Manager	Amy Clement
Assistant Stage Manager	Valeria Bettini
Sound Designer	Harry Johnson
Chief Electrician	Jack Berry
Costume Supervisors	Alice Ellen Brown
	Ellen Murgatroyd
Props Buyer	Catriona McHugh
Props Maker	Phoebe Thompson

Biographies

JANE ASHER | OLIVIA PENNINGTON
Jane Asher began her career as an actress at the age of five, and has starred in many iconic stage and screen productions, including the feature film *Alfie*, the TV series of *Brideshead Revisited*, and the stage version of *Festen*. Her recent stage appearances include Claudia in a new adaptation of Penelope Lively's *Moon Tiger* at Bath Theatre Royal and on tour, and Lady Catherine De Bourgh in *Pride and Prejudice* at the Regent's Park Open Air Theatre. Recent screen appearances include the feature film comedies *Death at a Funeral* (dir. Frank Oz) and *I Give It a Year* (dir. Dan Mazer), and Stephen Poliakoff's *Dancing on the Edge*. Later this year she will work on the second series of Emma Reeves' CBBC series *Eve* and she recently finished filming the movie *Burn, Burn, Burn* for Chanya Button and the NBC series *Crossing Lines*.

GEORGINA BEEDLE | EMILY PENNINGTON
Georgina Beedle's theatre credits include Belle in *Game* (Almeida); Alice (U/S) in *Peter and Alice* (Michael Grandage Company, West End); *A Good Boy* (Young Cut) and *Responsible Other* (workshop; Made By Brick). Television credits include *Silk* and *Casualty* (BBC); *Doc Martin*, *Vicious* and *Midsomer Murders* (ITV). Films include *Obsidian* (UFO Films) and *Petroleum Spirit* (Mirror Productions).

CLIVE FRANCIS | WILLIAM PENNINGTON
Clive Francis trained at RADA, and has worked extensively throughout his career in theatre, film and television. He was in the original BBC production of *Poldark*, Dennis Potter's *Lipstick On Your Collar*, several classic costume dramas, and more recently Mike Leigh's *Mr Turner*. His recent theatre credits include *Never So Good* (National Theatre); *Enron* (Noël Coward); *84 Charing Cross Road* (Salisbury Playhouse); *The Madness of George III* (Apollo); *Thark* (Park) and his one-man show of *A Christmas Carol*. He is also a successful theatrical caricaturist and has adapted several books for the stage; his most recent being Susan Hill's *The Small Hand*.

ALEXANDER HANSON | GILES PENNINGTON
Alexander Hanson is a two-time Olivier Award nominee, and mainstay of London's West End. His recent theatre credits include *Accolade* (St James); *Single Spies* (Rose, Kingston); *An Ideal Husband* (Vaudeville); *Uncle Vanya* (Chichester Festival Theatre); *A Little Night Music* (West End/Broadway) and the title role in Andrew Lloyd Webber's *Stephen Ward* (Aldwych).

TOM HANSON | SIMON PENNINGTON
Tom Hanson is a recent graduate from RADA. He made his professional debut as Hugo in *Posh* at Nottingham Playhouse. Roles whilst training include Jerry in *Betrayal*, Tony Lumpkin in *She Stoops to Conquer*, Sir Arthur Clarington in *The Witch of Edmonton* and Benedick in *Much Ado About Nothing*.

AMBER JAMES | AURELIA NDJEYA
Amber James trained at Guildhall. Roles whilst training include Nadia in *Burnt By the Sun* (dir. Joseph Blatchley), Maria in *Twelfth Night* (dir. Mike Alfreds), Medea in *Medea* (dir. Patsy Rodenburg), Celia in *As You Like It* (dir. Richard Goulding) and Eve Douglas in *Her Naked Skin* (dir. Christian Burgess). This is her professional debut.

NICK SAMPSON | SAMUEL PENNINGTON
Nick Sampson's theatre credits include *Great Britain, NT50, Othello, The Captain of Köpenick, Timon of Athens, Collaborators, Hamlet, London Assurance, His Dark Materials, Cyrano de Bergerac, Henry V, The Coast of Utopia, The Relapse, The Winter's Tale, The Madness of George III* (all National Theatre); *The Shawshank Redemption* (West End); *Romance, King Charles III* (Almeida). Television and film credits include *Downton Abbey, Silk, EastEnders* and *An Education*.

KATIE SCARFE | ALICE PENNINGTON

Katie Scarfe trained at LAMDA. Recent theatre credits include *Mercury Fur* (Trafalgar Studios/Old Red Lion) and *Season's Greetings* (National Theatre). Radio and television credits include *Holby City* (BBC); *Emmerdale* (Yorkshire Television); *Nunc Demittis, A Little Twist of Dahl* (BBC Radio 4).

ANNA WILSON-JONES | SOPHIE PENNINGTON

Anna Wilson-Jones' theatre credits include *Kill Me Now* (Park); *Life After George* (Duchess); *Dangerous Corner* (Garrick) and *A Midsummer Night's Dream* (Bristol Old Vic). Television credits include *The Life and Adventures of Nick Nickleby, Black Mirror, The Night Watch, Come Rain, Come Shine, Hotel Babylon, Switch, Lewis, Phone Shop, DCI Banks, Law & Order, Misfits, Ashes to Ashes, Time of Your Life, Sugar Rush, Afterlife, Midsomer Murders, Hex, Ny-Lon, The Vice, As If, Monarch of the Glen, Inspector Morse, Spaced* and *Wonderful You*. Film credits include *Take Down, Gladiatress, The Mother, Mrs Caldicot's Cabbage War* and *Domani*.

HAMISH BREWSTER | YOUNG GILES PENNINGTON

Hamish Brewster was a drama scholar at St Edwards School in Oxfordshire and whilst there had the opportunity to play a variety of roles including Romeo in *Romeo and Juliet*, David Girschfeld in *Rubenstein Kiss* and Robert Preston in *The Clearing*. He is a member of the NYT where he appeared in *Slick*. This is his professional debut.

OLIVER BUCKNER | YOUNG SAMUEL PENNINGTON

Oliver Buckner is a recent graduate of the Guildford School of Acting. Theatre while training includes Pastor Manders in *Ghosts*, Chris Keller in *All My Sons,* Macbeth/ Ross in *Macbeth*, Scamp in *Osteria il Fiasco*, Briggs/Vicar in *Light Shining in Buckinghamshire*, Father Michael/Goodman in *There Is A War* and Suffolk/Richard III in *Henry VI*. Workshop: The Freezies in Street Theatre for Natural Theatre Company. After this he can be seen playing Edek in the UK tour of *The Silver Sword*. This is his professional debut.

ANDREW KEATLEY | PLAYWRIGHT

Andrew Keatley studied English and Drama at Royal Holloway, University of London, and acting at Webber Douglas. His first play, *Colourings*, was produced at the Old Red Lion, Islington – and he was chosen by Time Out magazine as one of their 'Tips for the Top' in their annual culture review. Other plays include *Go To Your God Like A Soldier* (Old Vic Tunnels, London/Underbelly, Edinburgh); *Care* (Bush); *Why Don't We Multiply?* and *Weapon of Choice* (Theatre503). He wrote his most recent play, *Alligators,* on attachment at the Royal Court. His first feature film, *For Grace,* was filmed in March and April of this year.

ANTONY EDEN | DIRECTOR

Antony Eden trained at LAMDA. Directing and assistant directing credits include *Sweeney Todd, Kiss of the Spiderwoman* (C Venues, Edinburgh Fringe); *Sweet Charity* (Bloomsbury); *The Vice, State of Affairs* (The Stag Theatre, Sevenoaks); *Effie's Burning* (Soho); *Franny* (Landor); *Vanity Fair, Trumpets and Raspberries* (Royal Lyceum, Edinburgh, dir. Tony Cowney). Acting credits include *Yes, Prime Minister* (British Theatre Playhouse international tour); *Bedroom Farce* (Oldham Coliseum/Harrogate); *Springs Eternal* (Orange Tree); *Woman in Black* (West End/UK and international tour); *Taking Steps* (Oldham Coliseum); *Carrie's War* (No.1 UK tour); *Cider with Rosie, The Merchant of Venice* (Theatre Royal Bury St Edmunds/tour); *Voyage Round My Father* (New Vic); *Something Wicked This Way Comes* (National Theatre of Scotland); *The Glass Menagerie, Mrs Warren's Profession* (Lyceum); *Treasure Island* (Belgrade, Coventry); *Hamlet* (Bloomsbury); *Great Expectations* (Unicorn); *The Baltimore Waltz* (Caird Co./Floodtide); *Les Miserables* (West End). Television credits include *Derren Brown: Apocalypse* (Channel 4); *The Landlady, Kevin and Co, Kevin's Cousins* (BBC) and *The Bill* (Carlton).

ELLIE COLLYER-BRISTOW | CASTING DIRECTOR
Credits include: *Handbagged* (UK tour); *Arcadia* (ETT/UK tour); *Told Look Younger* (Jermyn Street Theatre); *Eldorado* (Arcola); *Tape* (Trafalgar Studios); *Blue Remembered Hills, Playhouse Creatures, Fred's Diner* (Chichester Festival Theatre); *Four Nights in Knaresborough* (Southwark Playhouse); *Fings Ain't Wot They Used T'be, Bernarda Alba* (Union); *This Is How It Goes, A Christmas Carol* (King's Head); *Much* (Cock Tavern); *Bright Lights Big City* (Hoxton Hall); *Buried Child, The Drowsy Chaperone, Buddy: The Buddy Holly Story* (Upstairs At The Gatehouse). As casting associate for the Ambassador Theatre Group: *The Ruling Class, East is East, Richard III, The Pride, The Hothouse, Macbeth* (all Jamie Lloyd Productions/Trafalgar Studios); *Women on the Verge of a Nervous Breakdown* (Playhouse Theatre); *Passion Play* (Duke of York's); *Dirty Rotten Scoundrels* (Savoy/UK tour); *Spamalot* (Playhouse Theatre/2015 UK tour); *The Rocky Horror Show, Tonight's the Night, Annie Get Your Gun, Blue/Orange* (all UK tours). As casting assistant: films – *Pimp* (Triple S Films) and *Legacy* (Black Camel Productions); television – *Come Rain, Come Shine* (ITV); *Hattie* (BBC2); *Off the Hook* (BBC3) and *When Boris Met Dave* (Channel 4).

JAMES PERKINS | DESIGNER
James Perkins' theatre credits include *Little Shop of Horrors* (Royal Exchange, Manchester); *Breeders* (St James); *Shiver, Lost in Yonkers* (Watford Palace Theatre); *Ciphers* (Bush/Out of Joint); *1001 Nights* (Unicorn/Transport Theatre); *Liar Liar* (Unicorn); *Girl in the Yellow Dress* (Salisbury Playhouse); *Microcosm* (Soho); *Dances of Death* (Gate); *The Fantasist's Waltz* (York Theatre Royal); *Stockwell* (Tricycle); *Carthage, Foxfinder, The Bofors Gun, Trying* (Finborough); *The Only True History of Lizzie Finn, Floyd Collins* (Southwark Playhouse); *The Marriage of Figaro* (Wilton's Music Hall); *The Life of Stuff, Desolate Heaven, Threads, Many Moons* (Theatre503); *The Hotel Plays* (Grange Hotel); *St John's Night, Saraband* (Jermyn Street Theatre); *Pirates, Pinafore* (Buxton Opera House); *Matters of Life and Death* (Contemporary Dance UK tour); *Iolanthe, The Way Through the Woods* (Pleasance, London); *The Faerie Queen* (Lilian Baylis, Sadler's Wells) and *The Wonder* (BAC). James created Story Whores, and he is an associate of Forward Theatre Project and one third of Paper/Scissors/Stone.

PAUL COLWELL | LIGHTING DESIGNER
Paul Colwell trained in theatre electrics at City of Westminster College, and lectures at The Royal Central School of Speech and Drama, specialising in lighting design, production lighting, technical and production management. Credits include: *You Can't Take It with You* and *The Revenger's Tragedy* (Southwark Playhouse); *Gates of Gold* (Trafalgar Studios); *Life on the Stairs* (Stratford Rex, London); *The Gigli Concert* (Finborough/Assembly Rooms, Edinburgh); *Born and Dead* (Glory House, London).

STELLA CHEUNG | ASSOCIATE LIGHTING DESIGNER
Stella Cheung is a Theatre Lighting Design student at The Royal Central School of Speech and Drama. She has worked with Teater Ekamatra, one of Singapore's longest established theatre companies. Lighting design credits include: *Push* by Sapphire (Catherine Alexander and Grainne Byrne) and *Titus Andronicus* (Andrew Bone). Stella is a recipient of the National Arts Council Arts Scholarship (Undergraduate) 2014.

GARETH SOWERBY | PRODUCTION MANAGER
Gareth Sowerby has worked in touring theatre since a young age, and started his West End automation career at age seventeen on *Joseph and the Amazing Technicolour Dreamcoat*. Other West End credits include *Wicked!, War Horse, One Man, Two Guvnors* and *Love Never Dies*. He was also heavily involved in the building of the theatres on Disney's largest cruise ships, as well as working on the production teams for a number of years for Disney in the USA.

AMY CLEMENT | STAGE MANAGER

Amy Clement has recently graduated from The Royal Central School of Speech and Drama with a BA (Hons) Theatre Practice: Stage Management Degree. She has previously interned with the Royal Shakespeare Company and worked as an ASM on *Sweeney Todd* in Harrington's Pie Shop. She also did a season at the Edinburgh Fringe 2014 with Theatre Tours International. After *The Gathered Leaves* she will be working with the English National Opera for ten months.

VALERIA BETTINI | ASSISTANT STAGE MANAGER

Valeria Bettini is currently in her second year in Stage Management at The Royal Central School of Speech and Drama. Credits include: *Red! The Wolf Slayer!* (Central, Stage Manager); *Design for Dance 2015* (Platform Theatre, Deputy Stage Manager); *Lady Windermere's Fan* (Central, Stage Crew); *The Bird's Song* (Central, Stage Manager); *The Dance Connection* (Youth Music Theatre, Barbican, Plymouth; Deputy Stage Manager); *Love and Information* (Central; Assistant Stage Manager); *London Walks* (Central; Head Stage Manager); *Novecento* (Etcetera, Camden Fringe Festival; Stage Manager); *Macbeth* (Rose, Bankside; Stage Manager).

HARRY JOHNSON | SOUND DESIGNER

Harry Johnson is currently studying Sound Design for Theatre at The Royal Central School of Speech and Drama. He has a background in music performance with a diploma in Orchestral Percussion and Drum Kit as well as experience mixing live music. Sound design credits include: *The Wolf Man* by Eddie Howell and *The Woyzeck Theory* by Rory Devlin (both performed at the Platform Studio Theatre, King's Cross) and *Trojan Women* for Actors of Dionysus (performed at Spruce Wood).

JACK BERRY | CHIEF ELECTRICIAN

Jack Berry is currently studying Production Lighting at The Royal Central School of Speech and Drama. Previous work includes *Market Boy* (dir. Dan Herd), *The Man of Mode* (dir. Phillip Franks) and *The Good Person of Setzuan* (dir. Nancy Meckler).

ALICE ELLEN BROWN | COSTUME SUPERVISOR

Alice Ellen Brown has just finished her second year of study at The Royal Central School of Speech and Drama on the Costume Construction course. She has worked primarily as a costume maker on productions within the university including *Lady Windermere's Fan* and *West Side Story*. Credits as a maker: *Peter Pan and the Designers of the Caribbean* (Bloomsbury) and *Treasure Trail* (Nutkhut).

ELLEN MURGATROYD | COSTUME SUPERVISOR

Ellen Murgatroyd is in her second year studying Costume Construction at The Royal Central School of Speech and Drama. She has worked on a number of in-house productions as a maker and dresser such as *The Low Road*, *Lady Windermere's Fan* and *The Twee Musketeers*. Professional credits include making for *Peter Pan and the Designers of the Caribbean*.

CATRIONA MCHUGH | PROPS BUYER

Catriona McHugh is currently in her first year of studying Stage Management at The Royal Central School of Speech and Drama. Credits include: *The Low Road* (Assistant Stage Manager, RCSSD); *Sweet Charity* (Stage Manager, Stratford-upon-Avon College), *Lysistrata* (Deputy Stage Manager, Stratford-upon Avon College); *Under Milk Wood* (Assistant Stage Manager, Stage2 Youth Theatre), *The Permanent Way* (Assistant Stage Manager, Stage2 Youth Theatre).

PHOEBE THOMPSON | PROPS MAKER

Phoebe Thompson has just finished her first year studying for a Prop Making degree at The Royal Central School of Speech and Drama. She has worked on a number of productions – most recently as one of three prop makers on *Market Boy* in the Embassy Theatre, designed by Sarah Beaton and directed by Dan Herd.

DEAD LETTER PERFECT

Dead Letter Perfect are a new company that seek to produce good stories, well told; they can be old plays – or new, big, small, neat or messy, no matter the flavour – we just want to be married to good story. For us, character lies at the heart of good story, and we seek to make writers and actors central to all our output.

Dead Letter Perfect would like to thank Jez Bond, JJ Almond and all at Park Theatre. PW Productions, Colin Blumenau and the Production Exchange, Stage One, Paul Lyon-Maris, Thea Martin, United Agents, ATG, Natalie Yalden and all at JHI Marketing, N9 Design, the National Autistic Society, Royal Central School of Speech and Drama, the Umbrella Rooms, the Haymarket Hotel, Adam Morane-Griffiths, Neil Adleman, Richard Keatley, Tony and Norita Eden, Marion Auer, Denise Silvey, Matthew Hellyer, Piers Nimmo, Patrick Chatterton, Brigit Forsyth, Robin Herford, and Mark Bentley.

ROYAL CENTRAL
SCHOOL OF SPEECH & DRAMA

UNIVERSITY OF LONDON

About The Royal Central School of Speech and Drama

The Royal Central School of Speech and Drama is a higher education conservatoire – a specialist college nurturing creative collaboration. Courses include acting, applied theatre, movement, musical theatre, drama and movement therapy, theatre and live performance, puppetry, scenography, actor and teacher training, voice, technical arts and production, and writing for stage and broadcast media. With over sixty academic staff, together with visiting artists and lecturers, Central has the largest grouping of drama/theatre/performance specialists in the UK, an active research culture and is a hub for the theatre and performance industries.

Central is HEFCE's only designated Centre for Excellence in Training for Theatre and is a federal college of the University of London.

Proud to support

The National Autistic Society

The National Autistic Society is the UK's leading charity for people with autism and their families. Founded in 1962, it continues to spearhead national and international initiatives and provide a strong voice for all people with autism. The NAS provides a wide range of services to help people with autism and Asperger syndrome live their lives with as much independence as possible. **www.autism.org.uk**

Park Theatre is a theatre for London today. Our vision is to become a nationally and internationally recognised powerhouse of theatre.

★★★★★ 'A spanking new five-star neighbourhood theatre.'
Independent

We opened in May 2013 and stand proudly at the heart of our diverse Finsbury Park community. With two theatres, a rehearsal and workshop space plus an all-day café bar, our mission is to be a welcoming and vibrant destination for all.

We choose plays based on how they make us feel: presenting classics through to new writing, musicals to experimental theatre, all united by strong narrative drive and emotional content.

Alongside a large number of world premieres – including *Daytona*, with Maureen Lipman, which toured nationally and transferred to the West End – and UK premieres – including *Yellow Face*, which transferred to the National Theatre Shed, we have presented thrilling first revivals such as Richard Bean's *Toast*, with Matthew Kelly.

★★★★★ '**Constantly compelling**' *Daily Telegraph* on *Toast*

We have welcomed over two hundred thousand visitors through our doors, but as we grow we're looking forward to developing our audience base, reaching out into the community locally, forging partnerships internationally and continuing to attract the best talent in the industry.

To succeed in all of this, ongoing support is of paramount importance. As a charity with no public subsidy, none of this is possible without the help of our Friends, trusts and foundations, and corporate sponsors. To find out more about Park Theatre, our artistic and creative learning programmes and how you can support, please go to **parktheatre.co.uk**

Park Theatre Staff List

Artistic Director — Jez Bond
Executive Director — John–Jackson (JJ) Almond
Creative Director — Melli Bond
Development Director — Dorcas Morgan
Assistant to the Directors — Amy Lumsden
Finance Manager — Catherine Barrow
Venue and Volunteer Manager — Naomi Dixon
Sales Supervisor — Niamh Watson
Theatre and Buildings Technician — Mat Eldridge-Smith
Theatre Apprentice — Bessie Hitchin
Duty Venue Managers — Barry Card
Androulla Erotokritou
Haroula Lountzi

Café Bar General Manager — Tom Bailey
Bar Staff — Slain Decamps, Camille Metier,
Roberto Javier, Sarah Pau,
Ondrej Blazek, Kyoko Aoki,
Nicola Grant, Emma Petusson,
Joe Hornsby

For Invisible Light
Press Relations — by Target-Live

President

Jeremy Bond

Ambassadors
David Horovitch
Celia Imrie
Sean Mathias
Hattie Morahan
Tamzin Outhwaite

Associate Artists
Mark Cameron
Olivia Poulet
Sarah Rutherford (Writer in Residence)
Charlie Ward

Trustees
Nick Frankfort
Colin Hayfield
Rachel Lewis
Chris McGill
Frank McLoughlin
Nigel Pantling (Chair)
Leah Schmidt (Vice Chair)

With thanks to all of our supporters, donors and volunteers

Park Theatre, Clifton Terrace, London N4 3JP
020 7870 6876 | parktheatre.co.uk

THE GATHERED LEAVES

Andrew Keatley

Acknowledgments

Antony Eden.

Hugh Ross, Nick Hern, Joyce Nettles, Sarah Bird, Rose Cobbe, Malini Ladd.

Philip Franks, ATG, Thelma Holt, Dafydd Rogers, Ellie Collyer-Bristow, Sarah Gimblett, Adam Speers, Chris Campbell, Annie McRae, Jerry Patch, Emily Hickman, Jago Irwin.

Sarah Liisa Wilkinson, and all at Nick Hern Books.

Dan Rebellato, Sebastian Armesto, Ali Taylor, Lisa Spirling, Caroline Steinbeis, Derek Bond, Brett Goldstein, Faye Ward, Adam Morane-Griffiths, Luke Parker Bowles, Paul Jacobs.

Sam and Boo Danby.

Dr Lorna Wing.

Deborah Willey.

The Keatleys and Duttons.

A.K.

4

Characters

YOUNG SAMUEL PENNINGTON, *sixteen years old*
YOUNG GILES PENNINGTON, *fourteen years old*
WILLIAM PENNINGTON, *seventy-four years old*
OLIVIA PENNINGTON, *William's wife, seventy-three years old*
SAMUEL PENNINGTON, *William and Olivia's son, forty-nine years old*
GILES PENNINGTON, *William and Olivia's son, forty-seven years old*
SOPHIE PENNINGTON, *his wife, forty-five years old*
SIMON PENNINGTON, *their son, twenty-two years old*
EMILY PENNINGTON, *their daughter, nineteen years old*
ALICE PENNINGTON, *William and Olivia's daughter, thirty-nine years old*
AURELIA NDJEYA, *her daughter, seventeen years old*

Note on Text

(…) signifies a pause for thought/words

(–) signifies interruption or change of thought

(/) signifies overlapping dialogue

This text went to press before the end of rehearsals and so may differ slightly from the play as performed.

ACT ONE

Spring, 1964.

A low sun. Some woodland on the fringe of a private property belonging to the Pennington family.

YOUNG SAMUEL PENNINGTON *and* YOUNG GILES PENNINGTON *are dressed in a somewhat peculiar fashion for teenage boys –* YOUNG SAMUEL *wears a dress shirt, a cravat, a blazer, trousers and has a bandage around his head;* YOUNG GILES *wears trousers, a shirt and a cardigan. They have fashioned a kind of rudimentary base – stools, a table, assorted bric-a-brac, several school exercise books and a wooden box.*

They are engaged in a scene of heightened drama. YOUNG SAMUEL *is sitting in a chair and is turned slightly away from* YOUNG GILES *– who approaches cautiously.* YOUNG SAMUEL *holds a plastic cup filled with water.*

YOUNG GILES. 'Doctor – some very strange things are happening. I feel we're in a very dangerous position; this is no time for personal quarrels.'

YOUNG SAMUEL. 'Meaning?'

YOUNG GILES. 'I think you should go and apologise to Barbara at once.'

YOUNG SAMUEL. 'I'm afraid we have no time for codes and manners. And I certainly don't underestimate the dangers if they exist. But I must have time to think. I must think. (*Rises from the chair, and walks away from his brother.*) Rash action is worse than no action at all. Hmmm?'

YOUNG GILES. 'I don't see anything rash in apologising to Barbara! (*Follows his brother to where he is now stood.*) Frankly, Doctor, I find it / hard to keep pace with you.'

YOUNG SAMUEL (*breaking character*). No!

YOUNG GILES. What… what / is it?

YOUNG SAMUEL. You did it wrong again.

YOUNG GILES. Did I?

> YOUNG GILES *brings out a piece of paper from his pocket – and looks at it.*

YOUNG SAMUEL. Yes. Exactly the same as last time. It needs to be like this: (*Adopting slightly different voice.*) 'Frankly, *Doctor*, I find it hard to keep pace with you.' Do it like that. Like I just did it.

YOUNG GILES. Does it really matter that much?

YOUNG SAMUEL. Yes. Yes it does; it matters very much indeed.

YOUNG GILES. Why though?

YOUNG SAMUEL. Because it's not the same otherwise.

YOUNG GILES. But why does it have to be *exactly the same*?

YOUNG SAMUEL. Because otherwise it's not the real *Doctor Who*.

YOUNG GILES. All right then. Sorry. I'll try and…

> *Once again,* YOUNG GILES *and* YOUNG SAMUEL *return to the positions they started in.* YOUNG GILES *takes a deep breath, and begins the scene again; from* Doctor Who: The Edge of Destruction (*original transmission date 8th February 1964*).

> 'Doctor – some very strange things are happening. I feel we're in a very dangerous position; this is no time for personal quarrels.'

YOUNG SAMUEL. 'Meaning?'

YOUNG GILES. 'I think you should go and apologise to Barbara at once.'

YOUNG SAMUEL. 'I'm afraid we have no time for codes and manners. And I certainly don't underestimate the dangers if they exist. But I must have time to think. I must think. Rash action is worse than no action at all. Hmmm?'

Short pause.

YOUNG GILES. Sorry, I can't remember what comes –

YOUNG SAMUEL. Aaarrrgghhh! No, no, no, no, no!

YOUNG GILES *removes the piece of paper from his pocket again, unfolding it and studying it keenly.* YOUNG SAMUEL *is visibly agitated.*

YOUNG GILES. I just… I forgot what I'm supposed to say next.

YOUNG SAMUEL. You say 'I don't see anything rash in apologising to Barbara. / Frankly, Doctor, I find it hard to keep pace with you.' Like that. Yes.

YOUNG GILES (*reading*). 'Frankly, Doctor, I find it hard to keep pace with you.'

Beat. YOUNG GILES *looks dejected.*

Sorry. It's not as easy for me to remember as it is for you.

YOUNG SAMUEL. It is easy.

YOUNG GILES. For you, Samuel. It's easy for you. For me it's quite hard.

YOUNG SAMUEL. No – it's easy.

YOUNG GILES. I am *trying* to get it right, Samuel. I promise.

YOUNG SAMUEL. But you keep getting it wrong.

YOUNG GILES. I know, I know, but can't you just… can't you just be nice about it? Please. Be kind. I'm being kind. I don't *have* to play *Doctor Who* with you, you know? You're the one who wanted to play *Doctor Who*, not me.

YOUNG SAMUEL. Play on my own then.

YOUNG GILES. Oh, don't –

YOUNG SAMUEL. I can do it better on my own.

YOUNG SAMUEL *takes the piece of paper from* YOUNG
GILES *and puts it into one of the exercise books before
putting the book into the wooden box.*

YOUNG GILES. Samuel. I wasn't saying that I don't want to
play any more.

YOUNG SAMUEL *wanders back to his starting point and
begins to re-enact the scene – but this time playing both
parts.* YOUNG GILES *speaks intermittently across this –
but* YOUNG SAMUEL *does not react; he is in his own
impregnable bubble.*

YOUNG SAMUEL 'Doctor – some very strange things are
happening. I feel we're in a very dangerous position; this is
no time for personal quarrels.' 'Meaning?' 'I think you
should go and apologise to Barbara at once.' 'I'm afraid we
have no time for codes and manners. And I certainly don't
underestimate the dangers if they exist. But I must have time
to think. I must think. Rash action is worse than no action at
all. Hmmm?' 'I don't see anything rash in apologising to
Barbara! Frankly, Doctor, I find it hard to keep pace with
you.' 'You mean to keep one jump ahead – that you will
never be. You need my knowledge and ability to apply it, and
then you need my experience to gain the fullest results.'
'Results? For good or for evil?' 'One man's law is another
man's crime. Sleep on it, Chesterton. Sleep on it.'

YOUNG GILES. I do want to play, Samuel. But it's not very
nice for you to keep telling me off – and do you know what,
it's actually not very fair either. It's really not my fault that
I'm not as good at remembering things as you. I think that's
very mean of you if I'm being honest. Because I try my best
to help you with the things that you aren't very good at, and
here you are just telling me off because you're better at
remembering things, and that's really not very fair if you ask
me. But if you really don't want me to play then you should
say. But I think you do. So you should say that. If that's

right. You should say that you want me to play with you if that's right. Because if you don't then I can always just go away. I can just leave you on your own if you prefer. If that's what you want then I'll just go away.

Short pause. YOUNG SAMUEL *resurfaces from his bubble.*

YOUNG SAMUEL. That was perfect. Did you see it? Giles? Did you see it?

Blackout.

ACT TWO

Scene One

*Set: the kitchen of a resolutely conservative country house –
very late-twentieth-century* Country Life *magazine – with a
clear preference for traditional rustic tastes over modern
stylings. An Aga dominates the cooking area, and the surfaces
are all perfectly presented and ordered. The ceiling is relatively
high – which is a feature of the house in general. There is a
fairly sizeable round table that has been the scene of much
early-morning broadsheet studying over the years, and a
comfortable leather armchair in the corner. A large clock hangs
high on one of the walls. A slim door leads to the walk-in
larder; a door upstage left that leads to and from the hallway –
and partially visible front door. There is another doorway
downstage right that leads into the conservatory.*

Thursday, 27th March 1997. Late afternoon.

GILES PENNINGTON *and* SAMUEL PENNINGTON *are
standing beside the table; on top of the table is a large cake
depicting a detailed representation of a country house. There is
a large cardboard box to the side of the cake.*

SAMUEL. It's my best cake ever.

GILES. I agree.

SAMUEL. It's even better than my Apollo 11 Command
    Module one.

GILES. Really?

SAMUEL. The side hatch wasn't right.

GILES (*trying to be supportive*). I don't know…

SAMUEL. The handle was too big.

GILES. I don't –

SAMUEL. But this cake is pretty much perfect.

Beat.

GILES. Now, you remember that we've already taken lots of photos of it, don't you?

SAMUEL. Of what?

GILES. Of the cake. Of this cake.

SAMUEL. Photos of the cake. Yes.

GILES. And I've already taken them to be developed, and we'll pick them up after the weekend.

SAMUEL. After the weekend. Yes.

GILES. And you know that William is going to cut the cake, all right? And people are going to eat the cake. You know that, don't you?

SAMUEL. Yes. That's why I made it. For William. For his birthday. Yes.

GILES. But we took the photos, so it's all right.

SAMUEL....

GILES. They're yours. To keep. Samuel?

SAMUEL. Yes.

GILES. So it's all fine.

SAMUEL. Yes, it's all fine.

GILES. And I tell you what; I think it'd be really great if you could be there when William cuts the cake. Don't you?

SAMUEL. Yes. Blow out the candles. Cut the cake. Yes.

GILES. Sing 'Happy Birthday'.

SAMUEL. Yes. Sing the song. Three cheers.

GILES. Hip hip…

SAMUEL. Hooray.

GILES. That's the stuff.

SAMUEL. Yes. That's the stuff.

   Beat.

GILES. So you won't try and stop him?

SAMUEL. No.

GILES. Do you know what I mean, Samuel? Do you know what I just said?

SAMUEL. No.

GILES. I'm talking about William cutting the cake.

SAMUEL. Yes.

GILES. So you won't try and stop William cutting the cake?

SAMUEL. No.

GILES. Really?

SAMUEL. Yes.

GILES. Are you sure about that?

SAMUEL....

GILES. Maybe we should take some Polaroids as well. Just in case.

   SAMUEL *points at the cake.*

SAMUEL. We're in there.

GILES. That's right.

SAMUEL. In the kitchen.

GILES. Uh-huh.

SAMUEL. Right there.

GILES. Yes. We're in the cake.

SAMUEL. We're not in the cake.

GILES. No.

SAMUEL. We're in the house.

Beat.

(*Pointing at different parts of the cake in turn.*) That's your room. That's my room. That's Alice's room. That's the master bedroom. That's the upstairs guest room. That's the downstairs guest room. That's the drawing room. That's the dining room. That's the hallway. That's the downstairs bathroom. That's the downstairs loo. That's the upstairs bathroom. That's the upstairs loo. That's the conservatory. That's the attic. And that's William's study.

GILES. You got it all.

SAMUEL. And that's the driveway. I decided not to do the barn or the garden because it would have just been too big.

GILES. I think you've got it just right. Plus, if you'd done the garden then we'd never have been able to eat it all.

SAMUEL. You could probably eat it all, greedy-guts!

GILES. Charming.

SAMUEL. You are a greedy-guts though. That's what William says; he calls you the family pig. He says you're a pot-bellied prize porker.

GILES (*with knowing resignation*). I bet he does.

SAMUEL. He does.

Beat.

GILES. Do you think that maybe there are giant versions of you and I standing outside looking at the house like we're standing over the cake?

SAMUEL *wanders over to the window and looks outside – and up into the sky.*

SAMUEL. No.

OLIVIA PENNINGTON *enters from the hallway; she has a sense of Home Counties style and presentation that is deeply considered and that belies her relatively advanced age. She is wearing gardening gloves and has a pair of secateurs in her hand.*

OLIVIA. Giles?

GILES *suddenly lurches into action – and quickly, yet carefully, covers the cake with a cardboard box.*

GILES. Sorry. The door was open so we just –

OLIVIA. I thought I heard a car.

GILES. William's not...

GILES *points out to the hallway animatedly.*

OLIVIA. William's not what?

GILES. Not... he's not about, is he?

OLIVIA. He's having a sleep.

GILES. Ah. Okay. Is he all right? He hasn't –

OLIVIA. He's just having a snooze.

GILES. Good. Perfect. Because we've brought the cake round, and we really want it to be a surprise.

OLIVIA. Can I see it?

GILES (*to* SAMUEL). Can Olivia see the cake?

SAMUEL *lifts the cardboard box – revealing the cake.*

OLIVIA. Oh, Samuel! Aren't you clever?

SAMUEL. It's the house.

OLIVIA. Yes. I can see it's the house.

SAMUEL. It has to stay in the box; it can't go in the big fridge.

OLIVIA. Right.

SAMUEL. It needs to rest at sixty-four degrees Fahrenheit.

OLIVIA. Shall we put it in the pantry?

OLIVIA *removes her gardening gloves and puts them – and the secateurs – on the kitchen table.*

SAMUEL. Sixty-four degrees Fahrenheit.

OLIVIA (*dismissively*). Yes.

SAMUEL. Be careful; it's very delicate.

OLIVIA. I'll be very careful.

OLIVIA *goes to pick up the cake – but stops a little short.*

Actually I think it might be a bit heavy for me. Giles?

GILES. Of course.

GILES *immediately intervenes, picks up the cake and carries it into the pantry.* OLIVIA *opens the pantry door for him as he goes.*

OLIVIA. How long did it take you to make?

SAMUEL. To make what?

OLIVIA. The cake.

SAMUEL. Oh… pretty much the whole of yesterday.

OLIVIA. Who was it that helped you this time?

SAMUEL. Janet helped.

Beat.

OLIVIA. Can I see your hands, please?

SAMUEL. I already showed Giles my hands.

OLIVIA. Well, I want to see them too, please.

SAMUEL *shows* OLIVIA *his hands.*

SAMUEL. Janet made me wear the gloves when opening and shutting the oven. I was very careful throughout.

OLIVIA *gives* SAMUEL *a little kiss on his hands.*

OLIVIA. Good boy.

GILES *returns from the pantry.*

SAMUEL. I want to check that you've done it correctly.

GILES. Wow. Thanks for the vote of confidence.

SAMUEL *passes* GILES *and enters the pantry.*

Right. So... about tomorrow; Alice's flight is due in mid-afternoon, which means we should comfortably be back here in time for dinner.

OLIVIA. That's good news.

GILES. Yes. Yes, it is. But the bad news is I'm going to need to drop my lot around here first before I head off / to the airport...

OLIVIA. Oh, Giles, that's not bad news.

GILES....so I'll aim to do that straight after lunch if that's all right with you.

Beat.

OLIVIA. Why don't we all just have lunch here?

GILES. Umm...

OLIVIA. It'll make everything so much easier. For you at least. Time-wise. So you'll be in less of a hurry. And it's no skin off my nose – we've already got enough food in this house to feed a small army.

GILES. You're already going to be spending most of the weekend cooking. Do you really want to add another – ?

OLIVIA. I'm thinking something cold.

Beat.

GILES. Shall we say one o'clock then?

OLIVIA. Lovely. And do you think you can pick Samuel up on your way here?

GILES. Well... it's going to be a bit of a squeeze in the back seat but... yeah, fine.

SAMUEL *returns from the pantry; he leaves the pantry door wide open.*

Everything all right in there?

SAMUEL. Yes.

GILES. And the temperature?

SAMUEL. The temperature is adequate. Yes.

GILES. Right. Well, that's a relief. So… we should probably make a move I reckon; otherwise I won't manage to get you back in time for Janet's Easter-egg hunt.

SAMUEL. You said that you would get me back in time for Janet's Easter-egg hunt.

GILES. Yes. And that's why we have to leave now. So we'll see you tomorrow, Olivia.

OLIVIA. Yes. At one.

GILES *exits;* SAMUEL *follows.*

See you tomorrow, darling.

SAMUEL. Yes.

SAMUEL *exits.*

OLIVIA *closes the pantry door, then takes a hotplate kettle from beside the Aga and starts to fill it with water from the tap.*

A car engine starts outside, followed by a few loud bursts on the horn. OLIVIA *looks up and out of the window. She waves – and then puts her finger to her lips in a 'please be quiet' manner.*

She finishes filling the kettle, and then places it on the hotplate.

WILLIAM PENNINGTON *enters; he is a well-preserved gentleman of very nearly seventy-five years of age. He is dressed very smartly even though he has no intention of leaving the house today.*

OLIVIA. Oh, you're up. Did you / manage to sleep at all?

WILLIAM. Who was that honking?

OLIVIA. Giles and Samuel. You just missed them.

WILLIAM. What did they want?

OLIVIA. Oh… just dropped in to say hello.

WILLIAM. Then why were they honking the horn?

OLIVIA. Samuel…

> OLIVIA *does not need to explain any further.*

WILLIAM. Such a repugnant noise.

OLIVIA. I'm making a pot of tea. Would you like some?

WILLIAM.…

OLIVIA. William? Cup of tea?

WILLIAM. No; not for me, thank you.

> OLIVIA *begins arranging items on a tray; a cup, a saucer, a teapot, some loose tea, a strainer, a teaspoon and a small jug of milk.*

OLIVIA. I told Giles to bring everyone round in time for a spot of light lunch tomorrow.

WILLIAM. I thought we'd agreed after lunch.

OLIVIA. Yes, but Giles has to be away to the airport early afternoon so it wasn't going to work. He said that they'll pick up Samuel on their way here.

WILLIAM. Well, at least that's one less thing to worry about.

> *Beat.*

OLIVIA. I've nearly finished now you'll be pleased to know; just the upstairs bathrooms to go.

WILLIAM. Olivia; how dirty can the upstairs bathrooms be? It's not like anyone has used them since the last time they were cleaned.

OLIVIA. They're a bit dusty.

WILLIAM. So they're a bit dusty. It hardly matters.

OLIVIA. It matters to me.

WILLIAM. Suit yourself.

OLIVIA. I will suit / myself.

WILLIAM. But it's above and beyond if you ask me.

Beat.

OLIVIA. Did you get a chance to finish the paper?

WILLIAM. Yes.

OLIVIA. Is that what's put you in a bad mood?

WILLIAM. I'm not in a bad mood.

OLIVIA. You're not in a *good* mood.

WILLIAM. Granted, I am not in the lightest of moods.

OLIVIA. Well, something's clearly wrong.

The kettle has now boiled; OLIVIA *removes it from the Aga and pours the boiling water into the teapot.*

WILLIAM. Piers bloody Merchant.

OLIVIA (*to herself*). I knew it was the paper.

WILLIAM. I mean the whole thing is a total bloody shambles! What is it – we're but weeks away from a General Election and on one side we've got Tim Smith doing the decent thing and resigning, and there's Neil Hamilton holding on for dear life like the bloody cowboy that he is. I mean, did nobody think to tell them that it might make sense for them to both walk the same damned path? Smith resigning is tantamount to admitting culpability. Good man. Fall on your sword – there's honour in that. But for Hamilton to hold his office and think he can just sweep the whole thing under the carpet is just pathetic; it's like trying to sweep the whole of Calcutta under a postage stamp using a feather – it can't be done. And now this idiot Merchant can't keep his hands off some young girl. It's ridiculous.

OLIVIA. I don't think it's as bad as all that.

WILLIAM. Not as bad as… It's happened so many times now that the media has a term for it, Olivia; 'Tory Sleaze'. They've designated a term for it. So it *is* that bad.

OLIVIA *puts the tea leaves into the teapot, then carries the tray over to the kitchen table.*

OLIVIA. Did you see the article in the paper about the Hillsborough boy?

WILLIAM. I did.

OLIVIA. Interesting, didn't you think?

WILLIAM. Yes. I imagine that's why they decided to put it in the newspaper…

OLIVIA. I just meant – in relation to neurology – you know, that they're managing to discover all these advances in –

WILLIAM. The boy was in a Persistent Vegetative State.

OLIVIA. I know, William.

WILLIAM. Well, that's hardly the same thing then, is it?

OLIVIA. I know. I was just… never mind.

OLIVIA *places her tea-strainer over her teacup.*

WILLIAM. Have you spoken to Giles about tomorrow?

OLIVIA. I already… yes.

WILLIAM. And what did he say?

OLIVIA. Oh… I thought I already told you.

WILLIAM. No.

OLIVIA. I'm sorry. Yes. He said that they'd arrive in time for lunch tomorrow.

WILLIAM. Typical Giles. Never one to miss a meal.

OLIVIA *pours herself a cup of tea.*

OLIVIA. He also said they'd pick up Samuel on the way.

WILLIAM. Right.

OLIVIA. And Alice's flight lands mid-afternoon, so they should comfortably get here in time for dinner.

WILLIAM. Fine.

Pause.

OLIVIA. You've taken your medication?

WILLIAM *has not registered this – or has tried not to register this. One of the two.*

I'm not talking to myself, William. Have you taken your medication?

WILLIAM. Yes. So, when are we expecting the boys?

OLIVIA. Well... Giles is picking up Samuel in the morning, and they'll be here for lunch tomorrow.

WILLIAM. Oh yes? Well, that's classic Giles; never one to miss a meal.

OLIVIA *puts her hand out towards* WILLIAM; *he takes it.*

Blackout.

Scene Two

Good Friday, 28th March 1997. Lunchtime.

The kitchen.

The sudden jarring sound of a door-knocker being firmly used.

More knocking. Loud and forceful. And then a doorbell being impatiently rung. And then more of the door-knocker.

OLIVIA *enters from the conservatory; she is wearing an apron.*

OLIVIA. I'm coming! I'm coming!

OLIVIA *strides through the kitchen to the front door, and opens it to reveal* SAMUEL – *who is carrying a small rucksack,* GILES, SOPHIE PENNINGTON, EMILY PENNINGTON *and* SIMON PENNINGTON. *The following exchanges are played out against a sequence of greetings: kisses on cheeks all round.*

GILES. I told you someone was coming.

SAMUEL. It's Olivia!

GILES. Hello.

OLIVIA. Hello, darling.

SAMUEL. I guessed it would be William.

OLIVIA. Have you got a kiss for me, Samuel?

SAMUEL. I sat in the front seat.

SAMUEL *gives* OLIVIA *a kiss on the cheek.*

OLIVIA. Lucky you. (*To* GILES.) Did you get here all right?

GILES. It was fine.

OLIVIA. Thanks again for picking your brother up.

GILES. Oh, it was / no problem.

SAMUEL. I got to choose the radio station.

OLIVIA. Come on through – or do you want / to bring bags through now?

SAMUEL. Sophie said just pick one and stick with it.

GILES. I'll get them in a bit. Where's William?

SAMUEL. Not to keep changing all the time.

OLIVIA. Oh, he's inside – somewhere. Hello, Sophie.

SOPHIE. Hello, Olivia; you look absolutely wonderful by the way.

OLIVIA (*taken aback*). I'm still wearing my apron.

SOPHIE. Even so.

OLIVIA. Well, do come in.

SOPHIE. Thank you.

> SAMUEL *walks in and sits straight down on the first chair in the hallway and starts reading his book* – The Northern Lights *by Phillip Pullman.*

> SOPHIE *enters and stands awkwardly on her own.*

OLIVIA. And who is this rather strapping young lad? He can't be any relation of ours – he's far too big and strong to be a Pennington.

SIMON. I'm very well thank you, Olivia. (*To* GILES.) And even better now since *you* owe me five pounds. Pay up!

GILES. Unbelievable!

OLIVIA. What?

GILES. Every time!

OLIVIA. What?

GILES. Simon bet me that you would mention something about his appearance within a minute of us being here.

SIMON. Don't worry, Olivia – I'll split it with you.

OLIVIA. But he's so very big – and broad – I can't help but mention it. Every time it takes me by surprise. I suppose I'm always expecting a five-year-old boy with a colouring book.

GILES. Well, he's still got his colouring-in book, I think.

SIMON. Yeah. Good one, Dad.

GILES. Well, I liked it.

Beat.

Actually maybe I'll get those bags now.

GILES *exits;* SIMON *follows him. Their exchange continues as they disappear towards the car.* OLIVIA *and* EMILY *continue the conversation at the front door.*

SIMON. I'll help; don't want you straining your back…

OLIVIA. You look absolutely stunning, Emily.

GILES. Are you saying I'm old?

EMILY. You look lovely too.

SIMON. You're quite old.

OLIVIA. I wish that were true, but thank you anyway.

GILES. Charming.

SOPHIE, EMILY *and* OLIVIA *are all gathered in the kitchen.* SAMUEL *is now sat down reading at the kitchen table.* WILLIAM *is standing in the doorway leading to the conservatory – he stares at* SAMUEL; *his appearance is seen by the three women.*

SOPHIE. Oh. There you are! We were wondering where –

WILLIAM. I don't feel very well all of a sudden. I'm sorry. I think I should probably have a lie-down.

SOPHIE. Oh. Would you like – ?

WILLIAM. Please excuse me.

There is an awkward moment. OLIVIA *does not know how to proceed. Everyone plays statues as* WILLIAM *heads through the kitchen towards the hallway. Suddenly* GILES *and* SIMON *return from the car with the bags.*

GILES. Now, I know it may look like we've packed a little bit heavy but that's because all of your birthday presents make up half of our luggage. I know you said you didn't want any 'things' and not to go to any trouble but –

WILLIAM. Didn't you hear me? I said I'm going to lie down. I said I'm not feeling well.

GILES. Oh. No. Sorry. I was outside getting the bags so I didn't... If you want I can have a look at... make sure it's not something to be worried about or... William?

As GILES *is talking,* WILLIAM *turns and begins the ascent of the stairs. The atmosphere is uncomfortable – for everyone other than* SAMUEL, *who has not even looked up from his book. There are some cursory glances swapped between the gallery as they watch* WILLIAM *reach the landing and disappear from view.*

Blackout.

Scene Three

Good Friday, 28th March 1997. Late afternoon.

Set: the drawing room of the Pennington household. There is a central fireplace, and various pieces of antique furniture – mostly Georgian – which lend the room a warm but formal atmosphere. There are two settees, and several armchairs of varying size. A grandfather clock looms tall in the corner; an antique piano is partially hidden by an ornate shawl. Various artworks – including several family portraits – adorn the walls. A television, positioned in the downstage-right corner of the room, various photo frames, and several magazines are the only modern signatures.

There is a door upstage left that leads to the hallway. The front door of the house is offstage (downstage left).

OLIVIA *is in the drawing room. She is looking at the room intently; after a long second she bends over and picks up a piece of fluff from the floor. She walks over to the bin and drops it in.*

GILES *enters.*

GILES. Right. I'm off to the airport. See you in a couple of hours or so.

OLIVIA. Drive safely.

GILES. Got anything exciting planned for this afternoon?

OLIVIA. Oh. This and that.

GILES. Gosh. This *and* that.

Beat.

How is he?

OLIVIA. He's having a little sleep.

GILES. I don't mean right now, I mean... I mean generally.

OLIVIA. He's the same.

GILES. Right. The same as what though?

OLIVIA. The same as he's been for a while.

GILES. Okay. But what exactly does that mean?

OLIVIA. Oh, I don't know, Giles. I'm not the absolute authority on your father, you know.

GILES. So, what, I should just ask him myself? How do you think / that's going to go down?

OLIVIA. I didn't say that.

GILES. Do you think I'm going to get an accurate honest appraisal out of William? I know this isn't... I'm only trying to help. I need you to tell me if there's anything new otherwise...

OLIVIA. He's fine. He's fine. He doesn't always remember everything, but then who does?

GILES. Has he been taking his medication?

OLIVIA. He's still calling it 'paint stripper'.

GILES. As long as he's taking it.

OLIVIA. He's taking it.

GILES (*pointedly*). And he's drinking less.

OLIVIA. He's drinking less.

GILES. It's important.

OLIVIA. I know, Giles. I've already heard it in stereo from William's doctors. I really don't need to hear it from you as well.

Beat.

GILES. And you? How are you doing at the moment?

OLIVIA. Yes, yes. All shipshape here.

GILES. Have you… you haven't spoken to Alice yet, have you?

OLIVIA. About…?

GILES. About William?

OLIVIA. Not yet. But we will. (*Sarcastically.*) Is that all right with you?

GILES. I'm not… please don't say it like that. It's just… I just thought that if I am going to pick her up then we might start talking about things so it's better I know whether she knows or not so I don't say the wrong thing and… you know.

OLIVIA. I think it's probably best not to mention anything anyway.

GILES. Well, I wasn't going to. It was just in case you had and… It's not like I *want* to… Oh for… I'm just going to go.

Beat.

Do you need me to pick anything up from the shops?

OLIVIA. I think we've got everything.

SAMUEL *enters the drawing room, closely followed by* SIMON.

GILES. I'm just about to go now, Samuel. You sure you don't want to come with me? Last chance to change your mind.

SAMUEL. Yes.

GILES. I'm picking up Alice from the airport.

SAMUEL. I know. Yes.

GILES. And you don't want to come?

SAMUEL. No.

GILES. You're sure? It's Alice. Your sister. Sure you don't want to come?

SAMUEL. I don't like airports. I like airplanes. But not airports. No.

GILES. Okay. Okay. See you later then.

SAMUEL *sits down on the floor by the settee.*

SAMUEL. Olivia?

OLIVIA. Yes.

SAMUEL *considers for a moment.*

SAMUEL (*in a slightly affected manner*). I'd very much like some jam tarts if I might be so bold.

OLIVIA. Well… you'll have to wait a while I'm afraid.

SAMUEL. How long is a while, please?

OLIVIA. About an hour or so.

Beat.

SAMUEL. I think I can wait a while.

OLIVIA. Then you're in luck.

SAMUEL. Yes. I'm in luck.

OLIVIA *exits.*

GILES. Do you know where your mother is?

SIMON. In the garden I think.

GILES. Well… when she comes in can you just tell her I had to head off, okay?

SIMON. Sure.

> GILES *makes a gesture to* SIMON *that essentially says 'Keep an eye on Samuel';* SIMON *nods dutifully, and* GILES *exits towards the front door.*

> So… what do you want to do?

SAMUEL. I'm going to read my book.

SIMON. Okay. What's it about?

SAMUEL. It's about lots of things. It's very hard to explain really.

SIMON. Sounds good.

SAMUEL. It is good. Yes.

> SIMON *looks around the room; his gaze rests on the television set.*

SIMON. Part of me wants to turn on the television. Is that going to annoy you?

> *Silence.*

> Samuel?

> SAMUEL *does not even register as he has opened his book and begun reading. But* SIMON *is still deliberating as to whether turning the television on might be a bad move.*

> (*To himself.*) It's just the television. It's not the gateway to hell.

> SIMON *turns on the television and sits back down; he holds the bulky remote in his hand. He changes channel once or twice, before sticking on a news report.*

TELEVISION NEWS JOURNALIST A. '…well, the implication it may have on the Conservative Party as a whole – and the leadership of John Major in particular – could be catastrophic.'

TELEVISION NEWS JOURNALIST B. 'I agree. For him to call a General Election before the findings of Sir Gordon

Downey's report are to be published – having previously insisted that such a course of events would categorically not happen – can only be seen to be, in my eyes at least, as damage limitation.'

SOPHIE *and* EMILY *have arrived back in the house, and are carrying some herbs and daffodils they have picked from the garden. Their attention is taken by the noise coming from the television in the drawing room; they are not aware that* SAMUEL *is in the room as he is hidden from view by the settee. The following exchange overlaps the latter half of the news report – so that they conclude at roughly the same time.*

SOPHIE. Simon!

SIMON *swings around – unaware that anyone had entered the room.*

SIMON. What?

SOPHIE. Did you turn that on?

SIMON. Yes.

SOPHIE. Then turn it off.

SIMON. Why?

SOPHIE. Because it's rude.

SIMON. How is / it rude?

SOPHIE. Just turn it off!

SIMON. I don't really see why / though?

SOPHIE. Because I'm telling you to!

SIMON *is nonplussed, but complies – turning the television off using the remote control.*

Thank you.

SIMON. I'm twenty-two years old.

SOPHIE. Excuse me?

SIMON. Telling me off like that; like I'm a child.

SOPHIE. Behave like a child, you get told off like a child.

Beat.

EMILY. I'm going to go and put these in the kitchen.

EMILY *takes all of the daffodils and herbs from* SOPHIE *and exits.*

SIMON. It wasn't like I was watching cartoons or something… I was watching *the news*.

SOPHIE. I don't care what you were watching. You don't just come in here and turn on the television.

SIMON. Christ! You're acting like I was taking a shit on the mantelpiece.

SOPHIE. Simon!

SIMON. What?

SOPHIE. Don't you swear at me!

SIMON. Right, so no swearing. No television. What, are we Amish all of a sudden?

SOPHIE. Don't get smart with me, Simon. I asked you to turn the television off and as far as I am concerned that is the end of it.

SIMON. Fine. Ridiculous. But fine.

SIMON *picks up a magazine that is on the low table in front of him; it is some kind of parish-news flyer. There is an uneasy silence; the kind of stand-off that follows an argument in which the next person to speak is either very brave or very foolish.* EMILY *re-enters, having successfully put the daffodils and herbs down.*

EMILY. Olivia says she's going to make jam tarts.

Beat.

Well, I think that's quite exciting.

Beat.

Has Dad gone already? Simon?

SIMON. Yeah.

EMILY. How long till they're back, do you think?

SIMON. He just left. So… couple of hours or so. I don't know.

EMILY. Think I'll probably go and start getting ready for dinner then.

SIMON. Two hours? You sure that gives you enough time?

EMILY *screws up her face at* SIMON, *then turns as if to leave – before turning straight back.*

EMILY. What do you think they'll be like? Aunt Alice and Aurelia.

SOPHIE. I don't know.

EMILY. But you must remember what Aunt Alice was like from before.

SOPHIE. That was such a long time ago.

EMILY. And…?

SOPHIE. Well… she was about your age then. I'm sure she's very different now.

EMILY. But what was she like then?

SOPHIE. She was very… young. Very headstrong. Very sure of herself. Very devil-may-care. I always… I always got the impression that she never really liked me very much.

EMILY. Why did you think that?

SOPHIE. Just… the way she was. Very disinterested in anything I had to say. Very superior, I felt. And yet, there she was, pregnant at twenty-one. And to a black man.

SIMON. Jesus Christ, Mum!

SOPHIE. What?

SIMON. I can't believe you sometimes.

SOPHIE. What? That's what happened.

SIMON. You can't say that; you can't say 'black man' like it's some kind of slur.

SOPHIE. But that's what it was, Simon. That's precisely what it was. I mean it was bad enough that she wasn't married – but it was doubly worse that... you know...

SIMON. Please don't say it again.

SOPHIE. He was... well...

SIMON. Mum!

SOPHIE. Well, you get the picture.

Beat.

EMILY. Have you seen any photos of Aurelia?

SOPHIE. Not recent ones.

EMILY. Is she black though?

SIMON....

SOPHIE. Well she's half-caste so / she's not completely black.

SIMON. Are you... Mum!

SOPHIE. What?

SIMON. I can't... Do you have any idea how racist that is?

SOPHIE. How is that racist? I'm not saying anything bad about them.

SIMON. About *them*?

SOPHIE. Yes. About them!

SIMON. People don't say half-caste any more, Mum. That's... you just don't say that. Not any more. It's pejorative. You say mixed-race.

SOPHIE. Fine. She's *mixed-race*.

SIMON. In fact you don't say anything you might have said in the past, or that they say in Bernard Cornwell novels or... Okay?

SOPHIE (*sarcastically*). Crikey, well, sorry for not being au fait with the appropriate terminology.

SIMON. You obviously didn't like her.

SOPHIE. I wouldn't say that exactly.

SIMON. Well, you're making it sound like everything that happened to her was… I don't know… some kind of comeuppance or something. Like what happened to her was completely disgraceful – and that she *deserved* it.

SOPHIE. It *was* disgraceful.

SIMON. In *your* eyes it was disgraceful.

SOPHIE. In *everyone's* eyes it was disgraceful.

EMILY. Why are you having a go at Mum?

SOPHIE. I'm just telling you the facts, Simon.

SIMON. Well, I don't think 'the facts' cover anyone in glory to be honest.

SOPHIE. Well, you have no idea what it was like. It's all very well to sit here twenty years later or whatever it is and say that having a baby with a black man is all well and normal, but it wasn't well and normal back then. It just wasn't. In fact it was a very big deal at the time. So rather than get all puffed up defending Aunt Alice – who you don't even actually know in case you had forgotten – why don't you get down from your high horse and realise that she caused a lot of people a lot of difficulty for a very long time.

SIMON. Christ! No wonder she decided to leave; hardly the dictionary definition of family support.

Beat.

EMILY. I don't get it.

SIMON. What? What don't you get?

EMILY. If she was pregnant then why didn't they just make her have an abortion?

SIMON. Oh, bloody hell, Emily!

EMILY. That's what they used to do, didn't they? Make young women have abortions.

SIMON. Am I the only feminist in the room?

EMILY. Why didn't they just do that?

SOPHIE. Because Alice didn't want to have an abortion.

EMILY. But why not?

SIMON. Are you really asking why a woman doesn't want to have an abortion? Is that really what you're asking?

EMILY. Uh! You can be such a condescending prick sometimes, Simon.

SOPHIE. Emily!

SIMON. But that is what you're asking, isn't it?

EMILY. No. I'm not. I'm asking why *Aunt Alice* didn't want to have an abortion. It's not the same thing, is it?

SIMON. Well, why do you think most women don't want to have an abortion?

EMILY. For lots of different reasons probably.

SIMON. But mostly because they want to keep the baby, don't you think?

EMILY. No. They might want to… they might decide to have it adopted. Or just be scared. Or maybe it's against their religion. Or whatever. Not everyone has a baby because they really wanted to have a baby, you know…

SIMON (*sarcastically*). Is that right? Well, thank you for that incredible insight into the mind of the pregnant woman.

EMILY (*sarcastically*). You're welcome. (*To* SOPHIE.) So, Mum, why did *Aunt Alice* not want to have an abortion.

SOPHIE. Well. I'm not sure… but I think because she decided she wanted to have the baby.

SIMON (*baiting* EMILY). I may be wrong but isn't that exactly what I said?

EMILY *picks up a cushion from an armchair and throws it at* SIMON – *but it misses. Instead it goes over the settee and lands by (or on)* SAMUEL – *who has until now been silently reading his book.* SAMUEL *automatically – and absent-mindedly – throws the cushion back.* SOPHIE *and* EMILY *are taken by surprise that he has been there throughout.*

SOPHIE. Oh my God! Samuel. I didn't see you down there. Are you all right?

SAMUEL *continues reading – he pays no attention to the others.*

(*To* SIMON.) Did you know he was down there?

SIMON. Yeah.

SOPHIE. Well, for crying out loud, Simon, you could have said something; I don't think what we've been talking about is really appropriate for –

SIMON. He's reading. He's dead to the world around him when he's got a book in front of him. (*To* SAMUEL.) Samuel?

There is no response from SAMUEL.

See.

SOPHIE. Well… (*To* EMILY.) I think you and I should go and put those daffs in some water before they start to dry up. And, Simon?

SIMON. Yes?

SOPHIE. Don't put the television back on.

SOPHIE *exits, quickly followed by* EMILY – *who rolls her eyes and shakes her head at her brother.*

SAMUEL *continues to read.* SIMON *looks around, picks up the remote control, and turns the television back on. The news is still on. He turns the volume down a few notches, and settles into the settee.*

TELEVISION NEWS JOURNALIST A. 'Do you think it's fair to say that these new scandals that have come to light in the past few weeks, the ones involving Piers Merchant and Sir Michael Hirst, and those from recent years, and I'm thinking of Stephen Milligan here, can only give further rise to the credentials of New Labour – and the credibility of Tony Blair?'

TELEVISION NEWS JOURNALIST B. 'I think large swathes of the voting public will have seen these recent press revelations as the straw that broke the camel's back – and the Tories are in such complete disarray that it's in danger of becoming a no-contest. Blair, meanwhile, is yet to put a foot wrong in all this really – and he is starting to look more and more like the man who will finally be bringing Labour back into power.'

Slow fade to black.

Scene Four

Good Friday, 28th March 1997. Late evening.

The drawing room.

The room has been overcome by the kind of arid silence that follows an ugly moment; eyes mostly avoiding contact with each other. WILLIAM *sits in his armchair.* OLIVIA *sits on one settee, with* SAMUEL *sat beside her.* SOPHIE *and* EMILY *sit on the other settee;* SIMON *sits on one of the other armchairs.*

SOPHIE. I'm sure they'll be here soon.

Beat.

I told him to get one of those phones; you know, one of those ones you can carry around with you. But no.

Short pause.

SIMON. Kind of wish I'd had a few more of those nuts now.

SOPHIE (*quiet but stern*). Simon!

SIMON. What?

OLIVIA. I can easily go and fetch some more.

SIMON. No, no, no, Olivia; I was just joking.

OLIVIA. It's not a problem. Or olives. Shall I get some olives?

SIMON. Honestly. I'm fine.

OLIVIA. I think we've probably got some of those Pringles that you always used to like. Shall I go and have a look?

SOPHIE. He's fine. Aren't you, Simon?

SIMON. I really was only joking.

SAMUEL. Pringles. Yes.

OLIVIA. You've already eaten all / those nuts, Samuel…

SAMUEL. Sour Cream and Onion. Yes.

OLIVIA.…so you'll have to wait for dinner now.

SAMUEL makes a small groan.

SOPHIE (*to* SIMON). Happy with your joke?

Beat.

SIMON. Do you mind if I ask what it is we're having for dinner?

OLIVIA. Salmon.

SIMON. Lovely.

Short pause.

I know that generally people eat fish on a Friday – or Catholics at least – so I was just wondering whether or not there might be any variation on Good Friday.

OLIVIA. Not that I know of.

SIMON. So salmon isn't like the *received* traditional fish for Good Friday or…

OLIVIA. I don't think there is one.

SIMON. Right.

Beat.

Is there a particular meat that people usually serve on Easter Sunday or…

SOPHIE (*sharply*). Simon…

SIMON. I'm just asking – it's all right to ask questions, isn't it? I mean, I'm interested, that's all.

OLIVIA. We'll be having roast lamb.

SIMON. Terrific.

OLIVIA. I think some people serve venison.

SIMON. Interesting.

OLIVIA. But we'll be having lamb.

SAMUEL. I'm not sure I'm really in the mood for lamb.

OLIVIA. Not now. On Sunday. Now we're having salmon.

SAMUEL. Ah. Yes… I'm not really in the mood for salmon either.

OLIVIA. Oh, Samuel…

SAMUEL. I think I probably ate one too many jam tarts.

Beat.

OLIVIA. I hope salmon is all right with everyone else for tonight.

All at the same time.

SOPHIE. Absolutely.

EMILY. Yes.

SIMON. No, I love salmon. I didn't mean that… No, salmon is wonderful. Perfect.

Beat.

OLIVIA. I've had to put everything in the bottom of the Aga to keep it warm… so I hope it isn't too dry.

SOPHIE. I'm sure it'll be fine.

OLIVIA. It'll probably be a bit dry.

SIMON. Oh, shush, Olivia. It'll be delicious.

Short pause. The awkwardness is getting close to unbearable.

EMILY. Can I please be excused? I have to…

OLIVIA. Yes, dear, of course.

EMILY *gets quickly to her feet and disappears through the drawing-room door, before heading straight to the lavatory in the hallway under the stairwell.*

Silence.

Maybe we should think about serving the food. William? I think that perhaps we should.

WILLIAM. We've waited this long. I'm sure we can wait a while longer.

OLIVIA. Then must we really sit here like nervous schoolchildren?

SOPHIE. It's fine, Olivia, really.

OLIVIA. It's nobody's fault that the flight was delayed.

WILLIAM. It's always somebody's fault, Olivia.

OLIVIA. Well, be that as it may, it's nearly half past eight so I think they would expect us to start.

WILLIAM. I'm not really very interested in what they would expect.

SAMUEL. I'm thirsty.

OLIVIA. Have a sip of your water then.

SAMUEL. I don't want water. I want some squash.

OLIVIA. You said you didn't want squash.

SAMUEL. I didn't want squash then. I want squash now.

OLIVIA. Fine; I'll go and get you some squash.

OLIVIA moves to get up.

WILLIAM (*to* SAMUEL). Drink the water if you're thirsty.

SAMUEL. I don't want water.

WILLIAM. There isn't any squash, so just drink the water.

OLIVIA. There's plenty of squash.

WILLIAM. He's not having any squash. If he's thirsty then he can drink the water. And if not then he can be quiet.

OLIVIA. I'm going to get him some squash.

WILLIAM. Sit down, Olivia.

OLIVIA. No. I will not –

WILLIAM. I said sit down!

The atmosphere becomes noticeably cold and overbearing. OLIVIA sits back down.

Is it so much to ask for? Is it really so much to ask for? For us just to sit here together and wait. To show some sense of the occasion. To think about more than just the food – and the drink – and the –

The doorbell sounds.

Finally.

SAMUEL. I really am very thirsty.

WILLIAM (*to* SIMON). Go and get the boy his bloody squash!

SIMON stands and exits; moving via the hallway to the kitchen.

OLIVIA *looks at* WILLIAM; *she realises that he is not going to leave his chair, so she rises and exits.* OLIVIA *makes her way via the hallway to the front door.* SOPHIE *sits awkwardly, while* SAMUEL *is quiet and still – lost in thought – essentially oblivious to the scene that is unfolding around him.* WILLIAM *sits stock still throughout; he and* SOPHIE *listen intently to what is about to happen by the front door.*

OLIVIA *opens the front door to reveal* ALICE PENNINGTON *and* AURELIA NDJEYA, *and behind them* GILES – *overladen with bags.*

They embrace; it is easy and natural. The following exchanges are played out in half-whispers:

ALICE. Sorry we're so late.

OLIVIA. It's fine. I'm just so glad you're here in one piece.

ALICE. Yes.

OLIVIA. Well, come in.

ALICE. Yes. Where is everyone else?

OLIVIA *sees* AURELIA. *She is a very striking-looking mixed-race girl.*

OLIVIA. Oh my…

AURELIA. Hello.

OLIVIA *gives* AURELIA *an almighty hug; it is full of enthusiasm and joy.* EMILY *has emerged from the lavatory and observes the scene – using the lavatory door as if it were a screen.*

OLIVIA. Are you well? You look very well.

AURELIA. I'm all right. Bit tired. And you?

OLIVIA. Yes. Yes. Fine. Just so happy you're here.

ALICE. Are you the one-woman welcoming committee?

OLIVIA. Oh. Everyone else is in the drawing room. Let's just go straight through.

ALICE. We thought you'd probably be in the middle of dinner.

OLIVIA. No. We were waiting for you, so…

ALICE. Oh. Okay.

OLIVIA *leads* ALICE *and* AURELIA *towards the drawing room.* GILES *stumbles through the door and places the bags in the hallway.*

I don't know about you, Aurelia, but I'm not that hungry, to be honest.

AURELIA. Not really.

OLIVIA. It's not a problem; I can do you a small plate if you like.

ALICE. Umm… actually I think I'm probably fine.

OLIVIA. Or a salad.

As they all enter the drawing room, WILLIAM *and* SOPHIE *are eagerly watching the doorway in anticipation of their arrival. There is a momentary silence.* ALICE*'s eyes rest on* SAMUEL.

ALICE. I know that face.

SAMUEL *looks up. He sees* ALICE, *and his face looks confused.*

SAMUEL (*a genuine question*). Is that… is that my sister Alice?

ALICE *walks straight over to* SAMUEL – *who is still sitting on the settee.* EMILY *has moved from behind the lavatory door and is now hovering behind the drawing-room door.* SIMON *emerges from the kitchen with the squash.* EMILY *sees him and gestures for him to wait; they listen together to what is happening in the drawing room.*

ALICE. Can I have a hug, please?

SAMUEL *has noticed* AURELIA *in the doorway.*

SAMUEL. Who's that?

ALICE. That's… that's my daughter. Aurelia. Do you remember her? She was my baby… she still *is* my baby. Do you remember?

SAMUEL. Yes. Aurelia. In the hospital. She was all sticky; like Venkman when he got slimed.

GILES (*to* AURELIA). It's from a film.

ALICE. Yes… Yes. That's right. That's her. Look at her now.

AURELIA. Hello.

SAMUEL (*to* ALICE). Where were you?

ALICE. Our flight got delayed. Sorry, everyone. I hope it hasn't been too much of a pain waiting for us to get here.

GILES. Partly my fault as well. I must have popped to the toilet when they finally came through, so they were walking around the blasted arrivals lounge for almost an hour until we found each other. Really annoying.

    ALICE *exchanges eye contact with* WILLIAM.

ALICE (*to* WILLIAM). Hello.

WILLIAM. Alice.

    Beat.

ALICE. This is Aurelia.

WILLIAM. I know who she is.

AURELIA. Hello.

WILLIAM. Yes.

    ALICE *looks anywhere else but at* WILLIAM. *She sees* SOPHIE.

ALICE. Sophie; look at you!

SOPHIE (*nervously*). Yes.

ALICE. You haven't aged a day I'd say. What are you – a witch or something?

SOPHIE....

ALICE. So... where are your two? They are here, aren't they? Giles said that –

SOPHIE. They're here. Somewhere.

SIMON *pushes past* EMILY *and enters the drawing room.*

SIMON. We're here. Hello.

SIMON *gives* ALICE *a kiss.* EMILY *shuffles into the room.*

ALICE. Wow! Look at the size of you.

SIMON. Yes. I'm all big and grown up. Apparently everyone is very proud.

ALICE. Ha!

SIMON (*to* AURELIA). Hi. I'm Simon.

AURELIA. Aurelia.

SIMON. And this is my sister, Emily.

EMILY. Hi.

AURELIA. Hi.

WILLIAM. Well. Now that we're all here – finally – I think that it's about time we sat down for dinner. It's already much later than we wanted it to be.

WILLIAM *rises, followed by* SOPHIE*;* SAMUEL *stays seated. There is general movement towards the drawing-room door.*

ALICE. Umm... To be honest, it was a long drive to the airport, then the delay, the flight, getting here... So if it's okay I think we'd rather just leave you all to enjoy dinner without us, and we'll just unpack – maybe have a shower – you know...

WILLIAM. I think all that can probably wait.

OLIVIA. William...

WILLIAM. The plan was for us to eat together – and so that is precisely what we are going to do.

Beat.

ALICE. But neither of us are hungry.

WILLIAM. Then don't eat anything.

Beat.

SIMON. Would it make sense for the rest of us to head through to the dining room and you can finish talking about this –

WILLIAM. No. It wouldn't.

GILES. I think that maybe –

WILLIAM. Yes, Giles? You have something to add, do you? You know, when you were gone I said that someone was probably to blame for your late return; I should really have known that your name was destined to be at the top of that list.

OLIVIA. William!

GILES. It's fine.

OLIVIA. It is / *not* fine.

GILES. I thought this might happen.

WILLIAM. I'm sure you did; after all, your contribution thus far has just been one pathetic *mea culpa* after another.

ALICE. Okay. Umm… before this becomes… why don't we go and freshen up and then join you all for dessert and –

WILLIAM. You can either come through and eat with us now – or not at all.

ALICE.…

WILLIAM. So are you coming through with the rest of your family for dinner or not? After we've spent God knows how long waiting for you to arrive.

ALICE. I don't know why this… I mean, it's not like we asked you to wait for us. If we'd known you were waiting then we'd have told you not to.

WILLIAM. And yet we waited! We waited for you. And do you know why we waited? Because your mother and I thought that it would mean something to all sit down together – tonight – for the first time ever. As a family. Even after everything that has passed. Does the significance of that even register with you? After seventeen years? And you would rather take a shower? Everyone is together for the first time *ever* and you cannot even bring yourself to sit down at the table? What does that say, Alice? What does that say about you?

Silence. ALICE is overwhelmed by the ferocity of this moment. The eyes of the room look downwards.

SAMUEL (*to* ALICE). Where were you?

OLIVIA. Not now, Samuel.

SAMUEL. All this time. Since you got the baby. Where were you?

Blackout.

Scene Five

Friday, 28th March 1997. Post-dinner.

The drawing room.

WILLIAM *is alone – and is watching television.*

TORY SPOKESPERSON. 'Well, you're talking like the public have already cast their votes. And they haven't.'

TELEVISION NEWS JOURNALIST. 'Well, really I'm talking in respect of the recent polls.'

TORY SPOKESPERSON. 'Well, with respect to you and to those polls, we are still several weeks away from this general election, so it's by no means a foregone conclusion.'

TELEVISION NEWS JOURNALIST. 'But you have to concede that it's looking like the end of an era for the Conservative Party.'

OLIVIA *enters. She hovers in the doorway.*

TORY SPOKESPERSON. 'Again… it's looking like nothing of the sort as of yet, so we're not in a position where we need to concede anything.'

TELEVISION NEWS JOURNALIST. 'But if these polls are / the reliable indicator of public opinion then – '

OLIVIA. Can you turn that off, please, William?

WILLIAM *turns the television set off with the remote control.*

WILLIAM. I know what you're going to say.

OLIVIA. Really?

WILLIAM. Yes. You're going to say that –

OLIVIA. No.

Beat.

WILLIAM. What do you mean, no? You don't know –

OLIVIA. No. It doesn't matter whether you know what I'm going to say or not, you deserve to have to hear it.

Beat.

WILLIAM. Fine.

OLIVIA. I hope you're pleased with yourself.

WILLIAM. You think I'm –

OLIVIA. I haven't finished. I hope you're pleased with yourself. Dictating proceedings like you did this evening – with no care or concession for anyone else in the room – you ought to be ashamed. You know you've got a houseful of people who are bending over backwards making allowances for you, and yet not only do you fail to notice; you fail to offer anything back.

WILLIAM. You think I offer nothing –

OLIVIA. I haven't finished! I want you to know I could have said this over the dinner table in front of everyone but I knew it would have incensed you even more so I had the decency to wait. So give me credit for that at least and listen to everything I have to say.

WILLIAM....

OLIVIA. Everyone has gone to bed. It's not even ten o'clock. They've all scurried off into their bedrooms because you behaved in such a way tonight that they'd rather hide away than be in the same room as you. So I hope you're pleased with yourself.

WILLIAM....

OLIVIA. I mean, nobody thought that this weekend was going to be easy – but I can't understand why you're determined to make it so hard.

WILLIAM....

OLIVIA. Why, William? I just don't understand why.

WILLIAM. Do you want me to answer that?

OLIVIA. I want you to shut up for once and show some bloody remorse.

WILLIAM. I'm not entirely sure what I should be showing / remorse for.

OLIVIA. Oh, don't play ignorant, / William.

WILLIAM. I barely said a word at dinner.

OLIVIA. And you think that's all right, do you? To just sit there like a bear with a headache...

WILLIAM....

OLIVIA. If it wasn't for Samuel then we would have all just sat there in an embarrassed silence.

WILLIAM. Well, thank God for Samuel then!

OLIVIA. You know what, William – you're right! Thank God for Samuel because although he finds it hard – in fact he finds it almost impossible – to understand the needs and desires of other people, he tries. Always. Without fail. What's your excuse?

Short pause.

WILLIAM. I had an idea of… of how I hoped today might go. It was all set up in front of me. And when it seemed to derail before Alice even arrived I… I felt that everything was slipping away from me and that I had to defend my corner.

OLIVIA. Your corner?

WILLIAM. Yes. My corner.

OLIVIA. What corner, William? Nobody was attacking you! If anything we're *in* your corner!

WILLIAM. It didn't look that way from where I was standing.

OLIVIA. And what about where everyone else was standing? Did you give even a second to think about that? About Alice. About what it must have looked like from where she was standing. Her first time back in this house since… And just a nod from you. A nod. You didn't even get to your feet. I mean, what sort of behaviour is that? And our granddaughter; looking at you for the first time in her life. I mean, you had the chance to welcome her into this family. Finally. Seventeen years she's been waiting to be a part of this family and what does she get from you; a pathetic mumble that tells her that as far as you're concerned she's pretty much nothing. And why? What; because they've arrived half an hour late for dinner and aren't hungry? Aurelia would have been within her rights to turn on the spot and write you off for ever. So I don't care what it looked like from where you were standing.

Short pause.

WILLIAM. Is that… Are you done?

OLIVIA. I've said what I wanted to say, yes. I don't know if I'm done. That'll depend on what you say now. And how you say it.

Beat.

WILLIAM. Seeing her here. Hearing her voice again. I didn't want it to but it took me back to...

OLIVIA. She's here now, William. But she won't be for long.

WILLIAM. I know.

OLIVIA. You've waited such a long time. I'm asking you kindly; please don't waste what time you have left.

Blackout.

ACT THREE

Scene One

Saturday, 29th March 1997. Mid-morning.

The kitchen. GILES *is making a pot of coffee.*

GILES *readies himself to begin pouring the coffee into several mugs. He fetches the milk jug and the sugar bowl. He then takes a long moment to savour being alone.*

SAMUEL *enters, gingerly carrying a matchbox.*

SAMUEL. Look what I found.

GILES. Oh. What is it?

SAMUEL. Look!

    SAMUEL *begins to carefully open the matchbox.*

GILES (*cautiously*). Is it a dead something?

SAMUEL. Just look!

    GILES *looks into the matchbox.*

GILES. I can't see anything.

SAMUEL. In the corner.

GILES. Where?

SAMUEL. There!

GILES. Oh!

SAMUEL. It's a ladybird.

GILES. Yes, it is.

SAMUEL. Do you know the Latin name?

GILES. No.

SAMUEL. Shall I tell you the Latin name?

GILES. Yes please.

SAMUEL. *Coccinella septempunctata.*

GILES. I think I prefer the name ladybird.

SAMUEL. What a lucky surprise! Because we're only in late March and the traditional time for ladybirds to populate an English country garden is not until April at the earliest. Because they are insects which go into diapause. Which is a lot like hibernation. So that's very lucky indeed.

GILES. Yes. Very clever of you to find one, I reckon.

SAMUEL. I just saw it. And that was that.

GILES. What are you going to do with it?

SAMUEL. Show it to everyone. I think that it's very interesting.

GILES. It *is* very interesting.

SAMUEL. And then I'll put it back where I found it.

GILES. I think that's probably a good idea.

SAMUEL. Because it's not actually mine to keep.

GILES. Yes.

SAMUEL. And it has things to do. Like eat, mate and pollinate.

SOPHIE *enters. She has wet hair and is slightly red in the face; she is fast and furious.*

SOPHIE (*to* SAMUEL). What the hell do you think you were just doing?

GILES. Sophie? What –

SOPHIE. What you just did is unacceptable. Do you hear me? Completely unacceptable.

GILES. What's… what is all this? What's / going on?

SOPHIE. He was outside the bathroom window – he was… he was trying to watch me while I was in there. While I was in the shower.

GILES. I don't think –

SOPHIE. I was naked, Giles. And I saw him! I saw him right up at the window – looking in.

GILES. Samuel? Is that true?

SOPHIE. Of course it's true. I bloody saw him.

GILES. Can you not swear at him, please?

SOPHIE. You were looking at me through the window, weren't you?

GILES. Please, just calm down; you're going to scare him.

SOPHIE. Maybe he needs scaring.

GILES. Sophie!

SOPHIE. Bloody Peeping Tom!

GILES. Please! I will handle this. Now, Samuel, I want you to tell me something – did you see Sophie when she was in the shower?

SAMUEL. No.

SOPHIE. You lying little –

GILES. Sophie!

SOPHIE. I saw him look at me. His face was right up against the fucking glass.

GILES. Sophie! He doesn't lie. He doesn't know how to.

SOPHIE. That's utter crap because –

GILES. No, it's not. It's not –

SOPHIE. Of course it's crap. Because I. *Saw*. Him!

SAMUEL. Do you want to see a ladybird?

SAMUEL *opens the matchbox again, and shows it to* SOPHIE.

I just found it outside. Which is quite lucky because they are not often to be found in March. Not in an English country garden.

Beat.

GILES. Samuel? Where did you find the ladybird?

SAMUEL. It was on the window.

GILES. Which window?

SAMUEL. For the downstairs guest bathroom.

GILES. And tell me something; when you were getting the ladybird did you look into the bathroom and see Sophie through the window?

SAMUEL. No.

SOPHIE (*trying to trap him with sweetness*). Not even for a second? Tell the truth now, Samuel.

SAMUEL. No. Was I supposed to? Nobody told me. I was concentrating on trying to get the ladybird into the matchbox. Did I get it wrong? Was I supposed to?

GILES. No, you weren't supposed to. It's fine. I tell you what, why don't you go and show the ladybird to everyone?

SAMUEL. Yes. Good idea, brother.

SAMUEL *wanders merrily out of the kitchen.*

GILES. I cannot believe you just did that.

SOPHIE. What? He was there. I'm not making it up.

GILES. I know you're not making it up, but for Christ's sake, Sophie, show a bit of restraint.

SOPHIE. What? It unsettled me.

GILES. Okay. I understand that. But to just accuse him straight out like that? That was really...

SOPHIE. Really what?

GILES. I just can't believe that you would even think that Samuel might do that.

SOPHIE. Part of me still thinks that he did do it.

GILES. He can't lie! What part of that don't you understand?

SOPHIE. No, that's not true. You always say that he does lie – occasionally.

GILES. He tries to lie sometimes – but he's not... he can't build a cover story, he's not capable of it, so it's so completely obvious when he tries that he might as well not even bother. And it's so rare anyway. And I know him. And I know when he's telling the truth.

SOPHIE. I knew you'd take his side.

GILES. What?

SOPHIE. I knew you'd defend him.

GILES. I'm not taking sides, I'm –

SOPHIE. Well, I don't see you lecturing him.

GILES. He didn't do anything wrong!

SOPHIE. So you say.

GILES. For the last time, Sophie – he cannot lie! Not about something like this. Which means he did not see you in the shower. Which means he has done nothing wrong. And which means we are currently arguing about the square root of nothing.

SOPHIE. You do always have to defend him though. You always have and you always will.

GILES. And why do you think that is? Why do you think I might want to defend him? It's because he's not as well-equipped as you or I to defend himself, and I'm his fucking brother. Okay? And on top of that, he's always under attack from people like you saying that / he's done something wrong; that he's a pervert, or he's backward, or he's simple...

SOPHIE. People like me?

GILES.... You do know what he was called until he was twenty-five years old? You know what they called him?

SOPHIE. Yes. I know.

GILES. They called him a retard. And that's not people on the street. Strangers. That was his doctors. That was his teachers. That was what the boys in his school all called him because that was what he was diagnosed as being. And he's not a retard. And he's not a pervert. He's actually very bright, and very wonderful, and very quiet and unassuming. And those are all things that I can happily defend – and I always will – because he's my brother. And I love him. And that is that.

GILES *has worked himself up to the verge of tears.*

SOPHIE. Well, if that's that then...

GILES *moves towards* SOPHIE *tenderly.*

GILES. I'm sorry. I really don't want to –

SOPHIE (*backing away*). Please don't...

GILES. I don't want to have any arguments. Not here. Not with you.

SOPHIE....

GILES. I know that things have been difficult recently... and I'm sorry. Last night with William has just left me... I just... this weekend has... I'm sorry. I just feel so...

Suddenly SAMUEL *enters, matchbox in hand;* GILES *and* SOPHIE *try to compose themselves.*

SAMUEL. I showed Simon and Aurelia.

GILES (*brightly*). And what did they all say?

SAMUEL. 'Wow!' and things like that.

GILES. Ha!

SAMUEL (*to* GILES). Your face is all red.

GILES. Is it?

SAMUEL. And your eyes are watery.

GILES *looks at* SOPHIE *for a moment.*

GILES. Sophie and I were having a 'holding our breath'
competition.

SAMUEL. Who won?

GILES. Sophie did.

SAMUEL. I thought maybe you did a sneeze. I just did a sneeze
earlier and my eyes watered a bit. Maybe it's the pollen. Yes.
I'm going to put him back on the windowsill. Do you want
to come with me, Giles – and you can watch me do it?

GILES. Yes. I'd like that. Thank you, Samuel.

SAMUEL. It's my pleasure.

SAMUEL *and* GILES *make to exit.*

(*To* SOPHIE.) What was your time?

SOPHIE. What?

SAMUEL. For holding your breath? What was your time?

SOPHIE. Umm…

SOPHIE *looks at* GILES – *he silently implores her to play
along.*

…Thirty seconds.

SAMUEL. Exactly?

GILES. I got twenty-eight seconds; Sophie got thirty. We timed
it on the clock.

SAMUEL. My go. Time me. Starting…

SAMUEL *takes in a big gulp of air and looks up at the
clock. As he finishes his inhalation he brings his hand down
to signal the start and then closes his eyes and screws his
face up.*

As SAMUEL *holds his breath,* SOPHIE *looks witheringly at*
GILES *and then begins to exit.*

GILES. I made you some coffee. It's on the side.

SOPHIE. I don't want coffee.

SOPHIE exits.

SAMUEL is still holding his breath.

After about forty seconds or so SAMUEL is still holding his breath.

GILES. You did it, Samuel. You won. You beat us both. Samuel. Samuel. You don't have to hold your breath any more. Samuel. Samuel.

Suddenly SAMUEL splutters as he exhales and then inhales quickly. He takes a moment to gather himself.

SAMUEL. Did I win?

Blackout.

Scene Two

Saturday, 29th March 1997. Early afternoon.

The kitchen.

ALICE *and* SAMUEL *are looking at photos.* SAMUEL *goes through the photos quickly, almost metronomically.*

ALICE. Slow down.

SAMUEL continues apace.

Stop.

SAMUEL stops; he looks up at ALICE.

Go back one.

SAMUEL goes back one photo.

Don't you want to know who that is?

SAMUEL. I like the ones with horses in.

ALICE. I know. But that's my partner. That's Hugo.

SAMUEL *looks at the photo of Hugo*.

SAMUEL. He has good hair.

ALICE. Yes. He does.

SAMUEL. It's big. And the beard. Like a lion.

ALICE. Yes.

SAMUEL *goes back to skipping through the photos*.

Do you want to know anything about Hugo?

SAMUEL. No thank you.

ALICE. Are you sure? You can ask me anything.

SAMUEL *thinks for a moment*.

SAMUEL. Yes; I'm sure.

AURELIA *appears from the hallway. She has been sitting out in the garden*.

AURELIA. You have to come and see this.

ALICE. What is it?

AURELIA. It's a... I don't know what the English... *une mongolfière*...

ALICE. A hot-air balloon.

AURELIA. But it's so close to the house you won't believe it. Quickly...

AURELIA *dashes back out*.

ALICE. Do you want to go outside and see the hot-air balloon?

SAMUEL. No.

ALICE. You sure? I think you'd like it.

SAMUEL. I want to stay inside.

ALICE. Have you ever seen a hot-air balloon before?

SAMUEL. Yes.

ALICE. Don't you like them then?

SAMUEL. I like them.

ALICE. But you'd rather stay inside?

SAMUEL. I'd rather stay inside. Yes.

   ALICE *puts all the photos to one side.*

ALICE. Can I ask you about where you live?

SAMUEL. Yes. You can ask me about where I live.

ALICE. What's it like? The place you live in.

SAMUEL. It's very nice indeed. I can decorate my room however I like.

ALICE. Brilliant. So how have you decorated it?

SAMUEL. Mostly with posters and maps and things like that. All over. Giles says that less is more but I like more. For me, more is more.

ALICE. So you have your own room?

SAMUEL. Yes. I have my own room. Yes.

ALICE. But other people live there.

SAMUEL. Yes. Other people. Yes.

ALICE. Is it a house or…?

SAMUEL. It's a house.

ALICE. And… and the other people – are they friendly?

SAMUEL. Sometimes they are friendly, yes.

ALICE. How many people?

SAMUEL. Eight people.

ALICE. That's a lot of people.

SAMUEL. It's a full house, yes.

Beat.

ALICE. Maybe Aurelia and I could come and see it.

SAMUEL. Yes.

ALICE. Would you like that?

SAMUEL. Don't move things.

ALICE. We won't move things.

SAMUEL. I have everything where I like it.

ALICE. I promise we won't move anything.

SAMUEL. Giles moves things.

Beat.

ALICE. Does Giles visit you?

SAMUEL. Yes. Every Monday. Six o'clock. Every Wednesday. Four o'clock. And Saturday… Saturday we're flexible on the time.

ALICE. That's good.

ALICE *takes a moment to have a good look at* SAMUEL – *who is oblivious to it.*

Last night you asked me something. Do you remember?

SAMUEL. No.

ALICE. You wanted to know where I've been.

SAMUEL. Oh. Yes.

ALICE. So I think it's only fair that I tell you, all right?

SAMUEL. It's only fair. Yes.

ALICE. Okay. So do you remember when I was at university?

SAMUEL. Yes.

ALICE. Well, when I was at university I fell in love with a man. He was very smart – like you – and very handsome – also like you. We were both very young. And a few months later I found out that I was pregnant.

SAMUEL. Yes. I know.

ALICE. And that was really scary because it was a surprise; neither of us had thought that was what would happen. But it did. And we didn't know what to do. And so we asked people what we should do – I asked my family what we should do. And do you know what they said? Giles said I should not have the baby; that I should have an abortion. You know what that is?

SAMUEL. Yes. You have to go to hospital.

ALICE. Right. And Olivia said that she didn't mind what I did. That she loved me whatever I decided to do. And then William said… William said… William said that I should have the baby. He said that if I had an abortion that I would regret it for the rest of my life. But William was so sad that I was so young, and that I wasn't married, and more than that he was so embarrassed by everything that had happened, that he decided that he didn't want me to be his daughter any more. And so I decided to have the baby. Because I didn't really have anything else left. And that's when I had Aurelia. And that's what happened to your little sister Alice.

SAMUEL. You should have just got married.

ALICE. Yes. Nobody really suggested that at the time, unfortunately…

SAMUEL. I'd like to get married I think. Sometimes I can be quite lonely, and I'd like someone to do things with. But Olivia says that not everyone gets married so I shall have to wait and see.

ALICE. Well… whoever she is, she'll be a very lucky lady.

SAMUEL *looks over towards the conservatory.*

SAMUEL. I went in a hot-air balloon.

ALICE. Did you?

SAMUEL. Yes.

ALICE. Really? When was that?

SAMUEL. We went around the world.

ALICE. That sounds fun.

SAMUEL. It was.

AURELIA *rushes back in.*

AURELIA. That was so cool. It couldn't have been more than fifty metres off the ground. They were waving back at me and everything. Why didn't you come out?

ALICE. We were talking.

AURELIA. Sorry. Am I disturbing you, Mum? Sorry, Uncle Samuel.

SAMUEL. I like your shorts.

AURELIA. Thank you. They actually used to be trousers but I cut the legs off.

SAMUEL. I like shorts. They are the most comfortable things to wear on my legs.

AURELIA. Then why don't you put on some shorts?

SAMUEL. William prefers it if I dress smart.

AURELIA. Haven't you got any smart shorts?

SAMUEL. No.

AURELIA. Well, we could always cut the legs off those trousers and then, hey presto, you've got your own shorts.

SAMUEL. 'Hey presto, you've got your own shorts.'

Beat.

ALICE. Do you want to cut your trousers up, Samuel? William and Olivia might not want you to.

SAMUEL. These aren't even my best smart trousers. So they can be my new best smart shorts.

ALICE. Even so, I think you'd better go and ask Olivia – and if she says that you can do it, then you can do it. But be careful.

SAMUEL grabs AURELIA by the wrist and leads her down the hallway. ALICE has a moment alone; she looks briefly in the cupboards and drawers. GILES enters.

GILES. That was seriously close.

ALICE. What?

GILES. The hot-air balloon. They must be landing somewhere around here. Maybe in the Hamiltons' grounds.

Beat. GILES surveys the room.

Oh. I thought Samuel was in here.

ALICE. Aurelia's just taken him off to turn his trousers into shorts.

GILES. What?

ALICE. Oh. They're going to ask Olivia first.

GILES. Right.

Beat.

Is he all right with her?

ALICE. Yeah. They seem to get on quite well actually.

GILES. That's… She seems…

ALICE. She seems what?

GILES. I don't know. Very poised.

ALICE. Is that a compliment or…

GILES. It's meant to be, yeah.

Beat.

ALICE. Do you want to know what Samuel just said?

GILES. Go on.

ALICE. He said something about going in a hot-air balloon once upon a time.

GILES. Did he?

ALICE. Yeah. He was all matter-of-fact about it.

GILES. Funny.

ALICE. But… I mean, he hasn't, has he?

Beat.

GILES. Oh. Right. Yes. I remember now. That must have been… well, he was Phileas Fogg and I was the… the other chap.

ALICE. You took him up in a hot-air balloon?

GILES. No. God no. We just pretended.

ALICE. Oh, right.

GILES. You know, like when we were children. We used to pretend. You must remember this; Samuel would watch something in a film or on television and he'd remember it all and write it down and then we'd recreate it.

ALICE. Oh. I thought –

GILES. So he can sometimes get a bit confused about what happens in his life and what happens in films and TV. Because when he's doing it it's like he's *actually* doing whatever it is he's doing. It's a bit like method acting or something. I'm told.

ALICE. Wow.

GILES. Yeah.

Beat.

ALICE. I've missed so much, haven't I?

GILES.…

Blackout.

Scene Three

Saturday, 29th March 1997. Late afternoon.

*The drawing room. The final stages of a game of Trivial
Pursuit. The entire family is playing, although* WILLIAM *is
dozing off, and* OLIVIA *is reading a magazine.* SAMUEL'*s
trousers are now shorts.* EMILY *is preparing to roll the die.*

SIMON. You have to be one of the worst rollers in board-game
history.

EMILY. Oh, shut up, Simon.

SOPHIE. Why do you two always have to antagonise one
another?

EMILY. He keeps trying to put me off.

SIMON. I don't need to put you off; you're naturally terrible.

EMILY (*recalling an earlier question*). Umm... How many
players in a netball team again? Is it six or seven? I forget.

SIMON. Fine. I got that wrong.

EMILY. Probably the easiest question so far.

SIMON. For you. You play netball.

EMILY. I think most people know how many people there are in
a netball team.

SIMON. Dad didn't know; and he used to watch you play the
damned game every week.

GILES. Good. I was hoping that might come up again.

SIMON. And anyway, I haven't actually noticed you getting
many right.

SOPHIE. Just roll the dice, Emily.

EMILY. Could you be any more competitive, Simon?

SOPHIE. A three or a four would be good.

SIMON. You're just bitter because we're winning.

EMILY *rolls the die.*

EMILY. Yes! / Three. This one is for a blue cheese!

SOPHIE. Good throw!

SIMON. You really need to get this right to / have any chance of winning.

EMILY. Yeah; you're boring us now, Simon.

SIMON. Pressure's on.

GILES. Blue cheese. That's funny. Because cheese is sometimes blue… None of the other colours really, although I suppose you could say that Red Leicester was an orange cheese.

SIMON. Thanks for that, Dad.

GILES. Just an observation.

EMILY. Blue question, please, Uncle Samuel. Everyone paying attention? Olivia?

OLIVIA *looks up from her magazine.* SAMUEL *withdraws a card from the question box.*

SAMUEL. 'What's the large African valley famous for archaeological discoveries?'

Beat.

SOPHIE. Anyone got any ideas? Because I haven't got a clue.

EMILY. Can I see the card?

SIMON. Why do you always need to see the card?

EMILY. To see how it's written down.

SIMON. There aren't even any unusual words in the question.

EMILY. Can I please see the card, Uncle Samuel?

SAMUEL *shows her the card.*

SIMON. Do you want me to tell you what archaeology is?

EMILY. I know what it is, thank you.

SIMON (*to* SAMUEL). Don't let her see the answer.

EMILY. I'm not trying to look at the answer.

SIMON. That's exactly what someone who was planning on looking at the answer would say.

Beat.

SOPHIE. Any ideas, Alice?

ALICE. Can you read it again please, Sam?

SAMUEL. 'What's the large African valley famous for archaeological discoveries?'

ALICE. It must be something along the Nile, I guess, but I don't know what it's called. Olivia?

OLIVIA. Yes.

ALICE. Do you know what it is?

OLIVIA. Oh no. I'm hopeless at geography. Sorry. No use at all.

ALICE. Aurelia?

AURELIA. Sorry. I've got no idea.

SIMON. Do you have an answer?

SOPHIE. This game really brings out an ugly side in you, Simon.

SIMON. I'll take that as a no.

EMILY. Shall we say something about the Nile? The Nile Valley? Is there such a thing? Or is that stupid... don't say anything, Simon!

SIMON. Is that your answer?

EMILY. Mum?

SOPHIE. I don't think we've got anything else, so...

EMILY. Aunt Alice?

ALICE. I don't think it's right but...

SIMON. We're going to have to hurry you.

EMILY. Shush!

SOPHIE. Just ignore him, Emily.

EMILY. Uh! It's so annoying; we keep getting all these obscure questions and they get questions about netball and 'what's the capital of Norway'.

SIMON. It's not actually that hard a question. And your answer is…

SOPHIE. We're going to say the Nile Valley.

SIMON. And the actual answer is – Samuel?

EMILY. So *you* don't know what it is?

SIMON. I've got an idea.

EMILY. Say it then. If it's 'not that hard a question'.

SIMON. Okay. I think it's the Great Rift Valley.

EMILY *looks hopefully over to* SAMUEL.

SAMUEL. Correct. The answer is the Great Rift Valley.

SIMON. I thank you.

EMILY. Ugh! You're such a smug bastard.

SOPHIE. Emily!

EMILY. What? He is!

SIMON. Do you even actually know what a bastard is?

SOPHIE. Please, you two! No more of that sort of language, okay?

SIMON. Apologies. Anyway. Our turn. Now if we get a four here, Samuel, then we can win the game.

SAMUEL *picks up the die. He blows on it, and then rolls it onto the board; it is a four.*

Yes!

WILLIAM *stirs – the noise has finally interrupted his nap.*

SAMUEL. It's a four.

SIMON. Now that's what I call good rolling.

EMILY. This is so unfair.

SIMON. How is it unfair?

EMILY. It just is.

EMILY *goes to draw the card out of the question box.*

SIMON. Wait, wait! You have to pick a colour and then ask us that question. And you're not allowed to look at the card first.

EMILY. I know what the rules are.

ALICE. Which colour shall we go for then?

EMILY. Definitely not green. They're the easiest.

SIMON. Plus Dad's a doctor, so…

GILES. Ooh… the pressure.

EMILY. Or blue or yellow. I don't know how but Simon the Spod seems to always know those.

SIMON. It's called education, Emily.

EMILY. Oh, shut up!

SOPHIE. And not orange because they're boys.

ALICE. I don't know.

AURELIA. Brown I reckon.

EMILY. Yes. Brown is art and literature, and they're a bunch of heathens.

SOPHIE. Olivia? What do you think?

OLIVIA *raises her head from her magazine.*

OLIVIA. What do I think about what?

SOPHIE. About the game. What colour shall we ask them?

OLIVIA. What colour did they land on?

ALICE. They're at the end and we have to pick a colour.

OLIVIA. Oh, I'm hopeless at this game. Do a brown one?

ALICE. Okay, let's ask them a brown one.

EMILY *draws the card.*

EMILY. Ready?

SIMON. Everyone ready? William? You with us again? You ready?

WILLIAM. What's the question?

EMILY. I'm just about to read it.

WILLIAM. Which colour?

EMILY. It's a brown; arts and literature.

SIMON. Ready, Uncle Samuel? This is to win the game.

EMILY *reads the question quickly to herself – adding to the tension – then aloud.*

EMILY. '"It was the best of times; it was the worst of times" is the opening line of which Charles Dickens novel?'

SIMON. Okay, I think / I know it.

WILLIAM. *Hard Times.*

EMILY *flips the card over to look at the answer.*

SIMON. Hang on, I thought… *Hard Times*? Are you sure?

WILLIAM. Yes.

SIMON. You've read it?

WILLIAM. I don't have to have read it to know the answer. It's one of the most famous first lines in literature.

SIMON. I was going to say *A Tale of Two Cities* – but I've never read either book.

GILES. I'm ashamed to say I've never read a single Dickens book. Not even at school when I was supposed to. So I'm no help at all I'm afraid.

SIMON (*to* WILLIAM). Well, if you're confident then –

SAMUEL. It's *A Tale of Two Cities*.

SIMON. What?

SAMUEL. It's *A Tale of Two Cities*.

SIMON. You've read it?

SAMUEL. Yes.

SIMON. And you remember it?

SAMUEL. Yes.

WILLIAM. He doesn't really know what we're talking about. He's just saying what you said to be difficult. The answer is *Hard Times*.

EMILY. Is that your official answer?

WILLIAM. Yes. *Hard Times*.

Beat.

EMILY. The answer is *A Tale of Two Cities*.

A difficult moment; the hackles of the room go up accordingly. The following dialogue tries to banish the awkwardness.

Unlucky. Anyway… / our go again.

GILES. Never mind. We're still in the lead.

SIMON. It's really just a stay of execution.

EMILY. We'll see about / that.

GILES. Come on, team! We'll get the next one.

EMILY. Time for a classic comeback.

SOPHIE. It's only a game, you two.

SIMON. Yes. That we're winning.

ALICE. I think everyone's taking things a little bit…

While the above dialogue is rolling, SAMUEL *begins talking aloud – almost in a trance. His voice slowly permeates the dialogue, until everyone becomes aware of what he is saying – and listen and watch in wonder.*

SAMUEL. 'It was the best of times, it was the worst of times, it was the age of wisdom, it was the age of foolishness, it was the epoch of belief, it was the epoch of incredulity, it was the season of Light, it was the season of Darkness, it was the spring of hope, it was the winter of despair, we had everything before us, we had nothing before us, we were all going direct to heaven, we were all going direct the other way – in short, the period was so far like the present period, that some of its noisiest authorities insisted on its being received, for good or for evil, in the superlative degree of comparison only.' That's *A Tale of Two Cities*.

WILLIAM *rises*.

WILLIAM. It's very impressive, Samuel. Remembering all those words; very impressive indeed. You're something like a parrot with the brain of a computer really, aren't you? But one has to wonder whether you have any idea what any of those words really mean.

GILES. Maybe we should just call it a draw and finish the game now –

WILLIAM. I haven't finished, Giles. Listening to Samuel reel off all those sentences made me think about something. And I want to tell you what that something was. For those of you who don't already know – which is most of you really, I suspect – I am not very well.

OLIVIA. William –

WILLIAM. It's fine, Olivia. I had made my preparations to do this last night but unfortunately events conspired against us and we ended up eating dinner in a veritable silence. So it's been sitting on my shoulder since then – like a monkey – whispering into my ear. Distracting me. And so now I must get it off my shoulder. Or get it off my chest rather. Get it off

my back. So what I wanted to say last night – what I am
saying now – is that apparently I am not well. Apparently I
have problems remembering things. Apparently I have
vascular dementia. I say apparently because I don't really
know what is actually wrong with me, and most of the time I
don't really think there is anything wrong, but I am reliably
told otherwise. In the last six months or so I have suffered
several minor strokes; nothing terrible – I'm still very much
me I'm sure you'll all be very disappointed to find out. But
I'm told that it is really just a matter of time before I might
suffer a much more serious stroke – and so that's why we
thought we should do our very best to get everyone here so
that we can spend a little time together as a family before it
is too late for me to really take part in something like that. I
know that I have not always behaved in a way that may have
endeared me to you; I am sorry about that. And I'm sorry to
say that I expect I shall inevitably continue in the same vein;
it's all I know. But I hope that we might be able to enjoy the
rest of the weekend, talk, sing, dance, be merry – perhaps
even be sad – and that we might be able to do all these things
together. I know it's not always that simple. But that's what I
wanted to say.

WILLIAM *sits back down. Silence.*

Does anybody have anything they would like to say?

Blackout.

Scene Four

Saturday, 29th March 1997. Late evening.

OLIVIA *is sat at the kitchen table*. GILES, ALICE *and* SAMUEL *stand around the room*. SAMUEL *is reading another book;* ALICE *has a glass of red wine in hand*.

ALICE. I can't believe that nobody told me earlier, that's all.

GILES. *That's* what you're upset about? You're / unbelievable...

ALICE. I'm still taking this in, Giles.

GILES. ...Because I thought the primary issue here would have been something to do with William.

ALICE. I know what the primary issue is, Giles.

GILES. Well, you seem to be fixating on the envelope and not reading the bloody letter.

Beat.

OLIVIA. We thought about telling you before and decided it was better to wait until you were here.

ALICE. But you decided to tell Giles?

OLIVIA. Giles has been here.

GILES. What – do you seriously think this is a case of playing favourites / or something?

ALICE. So I'm being punished for not being here?

OLIVIA. No, of course not.

GILES. And I'm a doctor, for Christ's sake; I'm in a position to help.

OLIVIA. Precisely. So we really didn't think there was anything to be gained from not telling him – in fact it was the opposite.

ALICE. So I'm being punished for not being here and for not being a doctor?

GILES. Why do you keep saying punished?

ALICE. Because that's what it feels like.

GILES. Really? Well, it's more punishing to know actually. I'd
love to have been you – happily gallivanting in the South of
France – oblivious to everything – and not had the worry and
the stress of the last few weeks. But maybe that's just me.

ALICE. Well, you've always wanted your head permanently in
the sand, Giles.

GILES. What's that supposed to mean?

ALICE. You know what it means.

OLIVIA. We agreed that we were going to tell you if you'd
decided not to come.

ALICE. Right. Well, that's a relief then. And if before that had
happened he'd had another stroke and died – you would have
told me *then*, would you? What would you have said *then*?

OLIVIA. We were trying to take everything into account; we
didn't want to scare you… and we wanted to wait for the
results of all the tests and find out what was really going on.

GILES. And anyway it's done now. So can we just put all the
'ifs' and 'buts' behind us, please?

ALICE. I just wish I had known earlier, that's all.

GILES. Do we really have to – you haven't been in touch,
Alice! You disappeared. So you don't have the right to have
any / complaints…

ALICE. I don't have the right?

GILES.…about decisions that have been made in your absence.
You can't just opt in and opt out whenever you want and
expect to be included when it magically suits you.

ALICE. What the hell has that got to do with anything? He's
my father too. You only have one father, Giles. I thought a
doctor might have grasped that.

GILES. Well, if you're so worried about your father then where the hell have you been for the last seventeen years?

WILLIAM *enters; he hovers in the doorway and watches silently.*

I've been here. I didn't just desert everyone when it suited me.

ALICE. What happened did not 'suit' me, Giles. / You don't even *know* what happened.

GILES. Well, whether it suited you or not, you did it anyway. To hell with everyone else. No explanations. No goodbyes. Just –

ALICE. Do you know what? I'm sick and tired of this. And I'm sick and tired of being painted as the bad person. So I'm sorry, Olivia, but I have to do this. William, I've visited my mother every year, sometimes twice a year, every year since I left. And every time I brought Aurelia with me. And we would meet somewhere and spend the day together. And we agreed to keep it a secret because we didn't want to… because we were making the best of a bad situation and if that was all that we had we didn't want to risk losing it. Because despite what you think, Giles, I do actually care. I'm not some kind of heartless bitch who moved away because she couldn't wait to wash her hands of her family; that's not what I am – and that's not what happened. So maybe you can stop talking to me as if your version of events is the gospel truth because I've had enough of your holier-than-thou attitude. I've had enough of it.

OLIVIA *does not know where to look or what to say.*

ALICE. I'm sorry.

WILLIAM. Is that true?

OLIVIA.…

WILLIAM. Olivia?

OLIVIA. Yes.

Beat.

WILLIAM. Good.

ALICE. Good?

WILLIAM. Yes. Good. Good on you. Both of you.

Beat.

ALICE. I can't tell whether you mean it or…

WILLIAM. I mean it.

OLIVIA. William…

WILLIAM. I often wish I had your temperament, Olivia. And your good grace. But I don't. I know that. But it is a great relief to know that you have them. And that you will always endeavour to use them. So good.

GILES (*to* WILLIAM). You should really have a glass of water and sit down.

WILLIAM. Look at us. Here. Together. You two squabbling while Samuel quietly reads a book in the corner; it feels exactly like old times. How rather wonderful. I can't tell if I'm in the present or thirty years in the past.

SAMUEL. My legs are cold.

OLIVIA. I told you I didn't think it was a good idea to cut the legs off those trousers.

SAMUEL. It was a good idea earlier. It's a bad idea now.

Beat.

WILLIAM. Samuel?

SAMUEL. Yes.

WILLIAM. Do you understand that I am ill?

SAMUEL. Yes.

WILLIAM. What do you think about that?

SAMUEL. I don't know. My legs are cold.

Blackout.

ACT FOUR

Scene One

Easter Sunday, 30th March 1997. Mid-morning.

AURELIA *is sat at the kitchen table; there is a pot of tea in front of her and two mugs. She is wearing a smart but conservative dress. She sits alone – and looks casually at the details of the room, letting her eyes rest on various family curios and objects that have been carefully positioned where they are found.*

SAMUEL *enters – carrying a small colourful box – the game Uno. He is dressed very smartly.*

SAMUEL. Got it!

AURELIA. Oh good.

SAMUEL *places the box on the table.*

SAMUEL. I will probably beat you.

AURELIA. That's okay. I don't mind.

SAMUEL *takes the cards out of the box and starts to sort the cards into some sort of order; he cannot do it particularly well.*

SAMUEL. I do normally win. But not always. It's a fair game. Not like noughts and crosses. In noughts and crosses I have worked out a system that means that nobody can ever beat me. I'm completely unbeatable. Giles says it somewhat takes the fun out of the game – but that could also be because he is a sore loser.

AURELIA. Tell me the rules then.

SAMUEL *starts picking up various cards in turn and showing them to* AURELIA.

SAMUEL. Right. This card is pick up four. This card means pick up two. This card means –

AURELIA. Pick up four what?

SAMUEL. Cards.

AURELIA. Right. From where?

SAMUEL. From the pile.

AURELIA. What pile?

SAMUEL. There is a pile of cards. You pick up cards if you cannot go.

AURELIA. Right. I'm a bit confused but...

SAMUEL. This card means reverse – but since there is only two of us playing then it doesn't matter. But it means reverse.

AURELIA. Reverse what?

SAMUEL. The order.

AURELIA. The order of what?

SAMUEL. Of who goes next. And this card means miss a turn. And this card –

AURELIA. Are there any instructions?

SAMUEL. Yes, but it's quicker if you listen.

AURELIA. Okay.

SAMUEL. This card means change colour. And all these cards are just cards with numbers on. Are you ready?

AURELIA. What's the point of the game?

SAMUEL. To get rid of all your cards.

AURELIA. Right. How many cards do we have?

SAMUEL. Seven cards.

Beat.

AURELIA. Okay. Let's just start and I'll pick it up as we go along.

SAMUEL. I'll show you what to do.

AURELIA. That's a good idea.

SAMUEL. Yes. So I'll deal the cards.

SAMUEL *gathers all the cards into a pile and begins to shuffle them in a very haphazard manner.*

Giles always says that I cheat and remember where all of the cards are, but I can't actually do that really. People think that maybe I can because that's what Rain Man does – but I'm not very good at it really. I don't know why. But just so you don't think I'm cheating then I'll close my eyes.

SAMUEL *closes his eyes, continuing his rudimentary shuffling. He then opens his eyes suddenly.*

I have autism. Do you know what that is?

AURELIA. I think so. A bit.

SAMUEL. Olivia says that it means that I am better at some things than others, but I think it means that I am not good at new things.

AURELIA. Right.

SAMUEL *gets ready to resume shuffling.*

Why do you call her Olivia?

SAMUEL. That's her name.

AURELIA. I know it's her name, but why don't you call her Mum? Or call William Dad?

SAMUEL. Because… because… because…

SAMUEL *closes his eyes again, continuing his rudimentary shuffling.*

If I close my eyes then I cannot know where any of the cards are. Unless I had learned to shuffle the cards in a special way, but I cannot even shuffle very well, so being able to do magic shuffling is not something I that –

Suddenly SAMUEL *loses control of the deck of cards; they scatter across the table. In this sudden moment of chaos,* SAMUEL *tries to grab the falling deck and knocks the teapot and/or the mugs over. Hot tea spills across the table – and begins to drip onto the kitchen floor. Some of it ends up on* SAMUEL, *and some of it on* AURELIA's *lap. Both of them instinctively jump to their feet;* AURELIA *looks around for some kind of cloth to clean up the mess.*

AURELIA. Oh. Whoops.

SAMUEL places his hand to his head in shock and pain. He then lets out a low, pained bellow. AURELIA watches him, unsure of what to do. SAMUEL starts to shake – his limbs whirl and his head jerks violently from side to side; he mutters odd words and dull sounds, sinking to the floor.

(*In French.*) Shit! Are you okay? Oh God. It's okay. It's okay. You don't have to… It's only a bit of tea. It's all right.

AURELIA *watches as* SAMUEL *continues to flail his arms; the noise and movement is disconcerting.* SAMUEL *– who now has his eyes shut – smacks himself firmly on the side of the face with the bottom of his clenched right fist.*

(*Shouting off.*) Mum! Granny! Uncle Giles! Someone, please!

GILES *enters. He surveys the scene in front of him. He slowly approaches* SAMUEL.

GILES. Woah! Samuel. It's all right, brother. It's all right. (*To* AURELIA.) What happened?

AURELIA. He knocked some of the tea over. He was shuffling the cards and then…

GILES. Okay. Can you go and get Olivia? It's all right. This happens sometimes. It's fine. Just get Olivia.

AURELIA *exits.* GILES *watches* SAMUEL *rock and moan; it is a fairly harrowing sight – even for* GILES, *who has seen it many times before. After a few moments,* GILES *has reached a position about a metre away from* SAMUEL –

and he extends his right hand out slowly towards SAMUEL.
WILLIAM *appears in the doorway, unbeknownst to* GILES,
and watches his two sons in silence.

It's all right, my brother. Everything's all right. You got a bit
of a nasty shock I reckon. But it's not important. As long as
you're all right then it's not important at all, is it? That's
right. It's not. And do you know why? Because I said so,
that's why. And I wouldn't lie about that, would I? You don't
lie to me – and I don't lie to you. That's right, isn't it? That's
what we say. So why don't you tell me that you're all right –
and then if you're all right then *everything* is all right. So are
you all right, my brother? Are you all right?

The sound of GILES – *his tone, his words, his presence –
goes some way to placating* SAMUEL. *The sudden
movements and sounds have gradually slowed until they are
eventually replaced with a gentle rhythmic murmuring and a
slight rocking movement back and forth.* WILLIAM *exits.*

I heard a good joke today. Do you want to hear it?

SAMUEL *rocks gently and murmurs.*

What do you use to cut the sea in half?

SAMUEL *rocks gently and murmurs. His eyes open.*

A sea-saw.

SAMUEL *rocks gently and murmurs. His eyes focus on*
GILES.

I like that one. That's a good old-fashioned joke for you. You
can have that one.

SAMUEL *puts out his hand and holds onto to* GILES'
*outstretched hand; this is the hand hold that has great
familiarity for both brothers.* OLIVIA *enters, quickly
followed by* AURELIA *and* SOPHIE.

OLIVIA. Is he all right?

GILES. He's fine.

OLIVIA. Is he wet?

GILES. No, I don't think so.

OLIVIA. So that's...

GILES. That's tea I think.

> OLIVIA *bends down beside* SAMUEL – *who is still making his rhythmic murmur.*

OLIVIA. Was it hot?

GILES. Umm...

OLIVIA. The tea? Did it burn him?

GILES. I don't –

AURELIA. No. I don't think it was hot enough to –

OLIVIA. Well, have a look at him, Giles.

> GILES *inspects* SAMUEL.

GILES. I think he's fine.

AURELIA. The tea went on both of us. It wasn't that hot.

OLIVIA. Right. Well then. Seems like everything is pretty normal, doesn't it? So let's get you to your room, I think. Don't you think, Samuel? Get you out of your damp church clothes and into your comfortable clothes. Yes? That sounds like an idea I think.

> OLIVIA *nods to* GILES, *who helps* SAMUEL *to his feet;* SAMUEL *does not actively move himself to stand, but he does not fight* GILES. *Once he is standing,* SAMUEL *shuffles off with* OLIVIA *and* GILES; *he is not sure of himself at all – he is almost walking as if controlled by someone else. The three of them exit slowly.* SOPHIE *and* AURELIA *watch silently.*

SOPHIE. Are you all right?

AURELIA. Yeah, I think so.

SOPHIE. It just happens sometimes. It's pretty much unavoidable really.

AURELIA. Oh. Okay.

SOPHIE. Did he hit you?

AURELIA....

SOPHIE. He punches sometimes. I don't think he realises what he's doing but...

AURELIA. No.

SOPHIE. Giles has been on the receiving end of quite a few smacks over the years, I can tell you that much.

AURELIA. That must be hard.

SOPHIE. He's attacked his mother before as well.

AURELIA. Right.

Beat.

SOPHIE. So he didn't hit you?

AURELIA. No. He just... no.

AURELIA *moves to start cleaning up the mess; she bends over to gather up the Uno cards from the floor.*

SOPHIE. Oh, I'll do that. You probably want to go and get changed as well. I know I would. I'll sort out the mess.

AURELIA. Right. Thanks. I mean, I don't mind helping though. I can always –

SOPHIE. It's fine. You go.

AURELIA. Thanks.

SOPHIE. Don't mention it.

AURELIA *exits.* SOPHIE *begins the process of cleaning; she picks up each of the Uno cards and puts them together by the sink, followed by the teapot and mugs (or pieces of). She then takes a moment to think about how best to proceed; she takes the marigold gloves and places them on her hands.* GILES *enters.*

GILES. Oh. Sophie. You don't have to –

SOPHIE. It's fine. I want to help.

GILES *walks over to the sideboard and grabs a length of paper towel from the dispenser. He folds it neatly and starts to dab the floor and table.* SOPHIE *looks under the sink – she picks up a cleaning spray and a cloth. The two of them work together to repair the kitchen to its previous state.*

GILES. He was doing so well. A full house. All the commotion. Seeing Alice again. Everything William's said. All sorts of things. And it's spilt tea that upsets him. It's –

SOPHIE. I really don't think I can keep this up any longer, Giles.

Beat.

GILES. Right.

SOPHIE. I'm sorry.

GILES. Your timing is…

SOPHIE. I know.

GILES. So… what do you… what does that mean, Sophie?

SOPHIE. I want us to stop pretending.

GILES….

SOPHIE. Don't you? It's just so exhausting that… I feel like I'm going to fall apart or something. Like my head's just going to fall off my shoulders.

GILES. Please. Please don't do this now. Not now, not here.

SOPHIE. I'm sorry. It's just –

GILES. It's Sunday morning; it's only one more day / and then…

SOPHIE. I know.

GILES. So can't we talk about this properly once the weekend is over? I've got enough to worry about without –

SOPHIE (*controlled*). I know. I know all the things you have to worry about, Giles. You've mentioned them enough times for me to know what they all are.

Beat.

GILES. You said it made sense to wait.

SOPHIE. No; that's what *you* said.

GILES. And you agreed with me.

SOPHIE. I didn't agree, Giles. I gave in.

GILES. You gave in? Right. *You* gave in. I'm sleeping on the floor in my own parents' house because you cannot even bear to share a bed with me. After nearly twenty-five years. But it was *you* that gave in.

SOPHIE. We don't share a bed at home, why should we / share a bed here?

GILES. Because you're putting me on the floor, Sophie! You feel more comfortable knowing that I'm on the floor than you would with me sleeping in the same bed. At least at home I have the luxury of the spare bedroom.

SOPHIE. You could have asked for separate bedrooms here – God knows your parents have enough of the damn things going spare.

GILES. And how do you think that would have gone down?

SOPHIE. It wouldn't have had to be a big… you could have just said it was because of your snoring.

GILES. My snoring?

SOPHIE. Well, it's what we / tell Simon and Emily at home.

GILES. So it's down to me to take the snoring bullet again, is it?

SOPHIE. If you're looking for an alternative to sleeping / on the floor then…

GILES. Why don't we say it's you that's got the snoring problem? Why does it have to be me that –

SOPHIE. Because we've already told Simon and Emily that you snore, so why / complicate the whole thing with...

GILES. Listen, I don't want my parents knowing that we don't share a bed, Sophie. Whatever cover story we happen to come up with.

SOPHIE. Why not?

GILES. Because they'll suspect that something is wrong.

SOPHIE. Something is wrong.

GILES. Well – whatever it is that's so fucking wrong – can we please just keep it to ourselves until after the weekend. For the sake of the children if nothing else.

SOPHIE. Neither of us are happy with the way things are. Not any more. That much is clear.

GILES. Well, I don't know what more I can do to make you happy, Soph. I don't know what –

SOPHIE. You can stop trying.

Beat.

GILES. Can we... can we please talk about this when we get home? I promise that –

SOPHIE. I've met someone, Giles.

GILES. What?

SOPHIE. I've met someone else.

Long pause. GILES *is hugely taken aback.*

SIMON *enters in a hurry. He sees* GILES *and* SOPHIE *and the remnants of the mess.*

SIMON. Woah! What happened in here?

SOPHIE. Just... just an accident.

GILES. Nothing terrible.

SIMON *walks confidently over and begins to immerse himself in the job at hand.*

SIMON. Right. Still. It's not going to clean itself up, is it?

GILES *and* SOPHIE *look at one another as* SIMON *drops to his knees and begins to wipe the floor.*

Fade to black.

Scene Two

Easter Sunday, 30th March 1997. Mid-morning.

The drawing room; ALICE *is sat on the piano stool. The shawl has been removed and the lid is open and* ALICE *is staring at the keys. Several moments pass.* GILES *enters.*

GILES. Oh. Sorry. I didn't think there was anyone in here.

ALICE. No, it's fine. I'm just sitting here.

GILES. Do you mind if I sit down? I fancy a sit-down.

ALICE. No.

GILES *makes his way over to the settee.*

GILES. We don't have to talk if you don't want to talk.

ALICE. I don't really mind either way.

Beat.

GILES. I think it probably needs tuning.

ALICE. Right.

GILES. I don't think anyone has played it for years.

ALICE. That's so sad.

GILES. Do you… do you have one at home?

ALICE. A piano? No.

GILES. So you haven't kept up?

ALICE. Not really.

GILES. So a bit.

ALICE. Barely even that.

GILES. That's a pity.

ALICE....

GILES. I only say that because you were so good. And because you worked so hard at it. I mean, you were always playing that piano really.

ALICE. It's funny, you know. When I was little I used to come and sit here when I felt like I wanted to be on my own. It wasn't like it was a decision I ever remember making – I would just find myself here. Like it was automatic. Like it was my safe place or something.

Beat.

GILES. Maybe I'll leave you to it.

GILES *rises.*

ALICE. No. Stay. Please.

GILES *sits back down.*

I spent so much time sat here. My body seems to remember so much, you know? Like I keep getting all these little flashes – tiny fragments of moments from my childhood. I don't even know if they're real – they're so hazy. Like really quiet echoes from the past that you think you might have misheard or made up.

GILES. It must be strange to be back.

ALICE. Like the angle of the grandfather clock; the face is impossible to see properly from here. I would always have to – (*Leans to the side.*) do this and crane my neck to check the time. I must have done that like a thousand times; my body still knows what to do. It remembers. The instinct is still there. The hours I must have spent here. Right here.

GILES. They nearly sold it. Did you know that?

ALICE. No. No, I didn't.

GILES. They had it valued. I think they were going to sell it or auction it or give it away. I can't remember.

ALICE. When was this?

GILES. A few years after you left.

ALICE. Did nobody want it?

GILES. No. They just decided they would rather keep it, I think.

ALICE. Oh. Why?

GILES. I'm not sure. One minute they were going to get rid of it and then they decided not to.

ALICE looks at the piano again. She puts her hands on the keys.

ALICE. It feels the same.

GILES. I'm sure.

ALICE. I wonder if it sounds the same.

ALICE presses down the middle-C key; it sounds strong and healthy.

GILES. Does it?

ALICE. I don't know yet.

ALICE presses a few notes gently; she is tentative like someone becoming reacquainted with something they love that they have not seen for a long time – something like a human coming across a wild beast that they once tamed.

After several moments, ALICE begins to play; it is a piece that she used to play as a child – 'Les Barricades Mystérieuses' by François Couperin. As she begins to play she becomes more and more ensconced in the act of playing, and the memory of playing; she is almost transported back in time to the piano-playing of her childhood. Her eyes are closed throughout.

During the course of the three-minute piece every member of the Pennington family arrives at the doorway – and enters to sit down or stand around the room – making sure to be absolutely quiet and reverential throughout. SAMUEL *sits next to* GILES *on the settee.* SIMON *and* EMILY *stand at the back of the room.* AURELIA *sits on the floor.* SOPHIE *joins her children by the back wall.* OLIVIA *and* WILLIAM *stand in the doorway.*

As ALICE *finishes the piece there is a long moment of stillness and silence. The scene is too much for* OLIVIA *who is overcome with tears.*

OLIVIA. Excuse me.

OLIVIA *exits. The significance of the moment is not lost on anyone. Except* SAMUEL.

SAMUEL. Again! Play it again!

Blackout.

Scene Three

Easter Sunday, 30th March 1997. Mid-afternoon.

SIMON *and* WILLIAM *are in the drawing room.* WILLIAM *is filling two port glasses from a port decanter.*

SIMON. Dad said that it would do you good, though.

WILLIAM. It would do him good. Glutton like him; fattest boy in his class until puberty hit and mercifully something shifted. You put away that amount of food then you have to do some kind of exercise after lunch or else you'll spontaneously combust.

WILLIAM *hands* SIMON *a glass of port.*

The reason I do not go in for afternoon walks is that the idea of walking round in a virtual circle is the preserve of the mentally incapacitated and the aimless. And I do not seek to be either.

WILLIAM *sits down on his favoured armchair.*

SIMON. Understood.

WILLIAM *has a large glug of his port.*

So… what do you say to a game of backgammon? Unless, of course, you'd rather not; I mean, I know how you *hate* losing.

WILLIAM. You say that like you actually have first-hand experience of beating me.

SIMON. I think you'll find that I won the last time we played.

WILLIAM. If you say so.

SIMON. Oh, I say so.

WILLIAM. Well – be a good sport and set the board up.

SIMON. Gladly.

SIMON *fetches the wooden backgammon board from the games cupboard, and begins the process of preparing the board for play.*

Do you want to be black or white?

WILLIAM. I've been meaning to ask you something.

SIMON. Black or white?

WILLIAM. It's somewhat off-topic.

SIMON. Okay. I'll be black.

WILLIAM. I want you to promise me that you will continue the family name.

WILLIAM *drains the rest of his port.*

SIMON. Say that again?

WILLIAM. I want you to promise me that you will continue the Pennington line.

SIMON. Is... is that a joke?

WILLIAM. No.

SIMON. Right... So... you're *genuinely* asking me to... to have... to have – I can't even say it – you're asking me to promise to have children?

WILLIAM. To have a son. Yes.

SIMON. I kind of wish I'd gone for that walk now.

WILLIAM *refills his port glass.*

WILLIAM. It would really have just delayed the inevitable. I've been waiting to have this conversation with you from the moment you were born.

SIMON. I don't know if I'm comfortable having this conversation actually.

WILLIAM. As the head of this family it is my responsibility to make sure that you register the importance of family, and of the family name.

SIMON. The thing is we're not only talking about names here; we are talking about actual children. Or does that fact escape you?

WILLIAM. Yes, Simon – I am well aware of that. Please don't be facile. You have a responsibility to this family which you should not take lightly. There is a lot that is staked on you being able to fulfil your duty.

SIMON. Duty? You make it sound so formal; so corporate.

WILLIAM. But that's what families are! Business! They're big business. The biggest! That's what they've always been – and you have to trade against it. The Middle East. The Far East. Africa. It's always been that way. Even here. In another era, less than a hundred years ago – no matter which family you were born into – you wouldn't have a choice; you would have just silently nodded at my decision, whatever it was, and then found someone suitable to provide you with a future bloodline – and not suitable for you, suitable for the family. So I want

you to think of all of the Penningtons that have gone before
you and recognise the debt that you owe them for the life that
you have inherited from them. Because that is what has
happened. You might think that you are your own man – and
that you can stride out in any which direction that might catch
your eye – but nothing you have is yours alone. Some part of
it was given to you. And you must pass that on. Your life is not
just yours. That is what I want you to acknowledge. And
maybe once you do that then you'll have the decency to
promise me that you'll continue the Pennington line.

SIMON. What you're asking of me is… I don't think it's a fair
thing to ask.

WILLIAM. I disagree. But even if you are right – I don't care.
And I'll tell you why. My brother died in 1942; he was
twenty-four years old. He was killed at El Alamein – he
served under Montgomery. I was twenty at the time, and also
serving my country. I remember the moment I was told. My
grandfather told me. Right here. In this very room. I
remember it as if it was yesterday. I was on leave and he sat
me down and told me that Nicholas had been killed. I am not
ashamed to tell you that I cried inconsolably. In spite of this
he proceeded to tell me that the future of the Pennington
name lay solely with me. So I went back to war with the
knowledge that I was no longer fighting just for my country
– or for myself. So I have sat in your seat. And I hope that
one day you will sit in mine. Whether it is fair or not.

SIMON. What will happen will happen. I can't say any more
than that.

Beat.

WILLIAM. I am meeting with my solicitor next week. It is my
intention to specify that any of my estate passed on to you
will only be done so on the proviso that you have a male
heir. Otherwise it will be forfeited to charity. Is that clear?

SIMON. Forfeited? Are you being serious?

WILLIAM. The Pennington line can be traced from you all the
way back to the eleventh century. Do you know how rare

that is these days? I'll bet your mother's family can't trace
their lineage back half as far as that. A quarter even.

SIMON. Please don't bring my mother's side of the family into
all this.

WILLIAM. We Penningtons have survived everything that
history has had to throw at us and we are still here. Still
standing. Still walking tall. And you – Simon – carry the
weight of that history squarely on your Pennington
shoulders. And it is yours to carry alone.

SIMON *walks briskly towards the door.*

Life is hard. And sometimes you have to ask – demand –
uncomfortable things of other people. Anybody who seeks
comfort over commitment is likely to end up on the losing
side. Comfort very soon becomes indulgence, indulgence
becomes laziness, and laziness loves a loser like a dog loves
the fireside. It's that simple.

SIMON *turns away from* WILLIAM, *ready to exit.*

If you leave the room now then I'll be chalking this game up
as a win for me.

SIMON *hovers for a moment, weighing up his options.*

SIMON. How did you... actually, do you know what, forget it.

WILLIAM. No, go on. Don't buckle. Tell me what you think.
Tell me what –

SIMON. Is it fun?

WILLIAM. Is what fun?

SIMON. Bursting other people's balloons.

WILLIAM. Nothing could be further from the truth.

SIMON. Then why do it?

WILLIAM. Because, Simon, I'm a realist. Because I haven't
got the time or the energy to entertain anything other than the
world in front of me.

SIMON. I think you're wrong.

WILLIAM. Of course you do.

SIMON. I don't think you see the world in front of you at all. I think you see a world from fifty years ago, and you've become a slave to it. You can't escape its thrall. But that world isn't here any more. It's just a shadow. Just like the rest of the past. It's gone, and what's left is completely different. But you can't see any of it. So even though you'll probably just disregard this challenge to your beliefs in your classic time-honoured way, please know – in black and white, like these bloody backgammon pieces – that you are wrong. About lots of things. And that even though you may hate losing – you may even hate it more than the rest of us – you might want to learn how to swallow it before it swallows you.

WILLIAM. Are you really trying to school me on the ways of the world? You've barely found a place to put your little mortarboard and suddenly you're picking up the chalk and dictating lessons. You may well puff out your chest and seek to display your Oxford University plumage but let me tell you something that is not on the syllabus; you know nothing of time. Nothing at all. I have lived long enough to see the unknown unfold in front of my eyes. I have watched it turn from nothing into something. Because I have spent time – I have spent nearly all of my time. And that time has taken me all over the world, and I have mapped myself accordingly. I've seen death up close, I've felt it grab me by the throat and then let me go. I've brought death to people. Do you understand? I delivered them there. And I've lost people that I loved. I have lived all of that – and many times over. You talk of challenging me. Challenging my point of view. My point of view is the product of challenge; I've been challenged all my life. What can you say? What can *you* say?

Blackout.

Scene Four

Easter Sunday, 30th March 1997. Late afternoon.

OLIVIA *and* ALICE *are in the kitchen.* ALICE *holds a mixing bowl; she swirls a finger around the inside and then removes it – licking her finger clean.*

OLIVIA. She was like a hawk. She'd make this noise as well, like a squawk, like '*araauu*' if she saw me think about eating it. But then at the end she'd let me lick my hands clean. All I could think about all the way through was getting to the end so I could eat the dough. And I'd always make sure that I had enough of the mixture on my hands at the end – but not so much that my grandmother would notice. So I'd have to try and get it just right; not make it obvious what I was doing. I asked her about it – when I was a bit older – and she told me that she was trying to teach me patience; that 'good things come to those who wait'. But it didn't work. I mean, I learnt patience. I think. Somewhere along the way. But making cookies with my grandmother – that's where I learnt how to balance large amounts of dough on my hands.

ALICE. It's a very important skill to master.

OLIVIA. Do you know what I really learned from making biscuits with my grandmother?

ALICE. No.

OLIVIA. How to get away with things even when someone is watching you.

ALICE. Are you talking about William?

OLIVIA. Yes and no. Maybe we should sit down; have a proper talk.

OLIVIA *gestures for* ALICE *to sit down – then she wanders over to the kitchen door, and gently closes it.*

Probably best to do this in private.

ALICE. What's going on? You're scaring me slightly.

OLIVIA *makes her way over to the table; they both sit.*

What's this about?

OLIVIA. I know that I neglected you. When you were a little girl. I know that I neglected you.

ALICE. I don't...

OLIVIA. It's all right. It's true. You shouldn't deny it; it'll just make it worse.

Beat.

ALICE. Why are you telling me this?

OLIVIA. Because I want you to know that I see it; that I'm not sitting here under the illusion that I am the world's greatest mother.

ALICE....

OLIVIA. It's not easy for me to say this to you; I hope you realise that.

ALICE. You don't have to say anything.

OLIVIA. I do. I feel like I do, you see. Because I paid too much attention to Samuel – I know I did –

ALICE. You had to.

OLIVIA. I was just so worried about him. All the time. I still am. It sounds silly to say that but I am. It's what I think about. All the time. Even when I'm thinking about something else, he's on my mind somehow. I can't seem to stop myself.

ALICE. I know.

OLIVIA. I used to lie awake at night – this is most nights – and think about what might lie in store for him. What sort of life he might be able to have.

ALICE. He's got a great life.

OLIVIA. And what might end up happening to him once... once I was no longer there to look after him.

ALICE. Right.

OLIVIA. Because really he's just the perfect victim, isn't he? If something were to happen to him then he's not always able to communicate what that thing is and…

ALICE. You don't have to –

OLIVIA. And I always just wanted – hoped even – that you and Giles would be fine.

ALICE. We were fine.

OLIVIA. To just magically be fine. I just wanted everyone to be fine. And one thing that seemed to make it all right – in my mind at least – was the fact that William always gave you so much attention. So…

OLIVIA *and* ALICE *are both choking back the beginnings of tears.*

ALICE. Mum…

OLIVIA. I'm sorry.

ALICE. It's all right.

OLIVIA. I think it's having everyone in the house. I've been on the verge of tears constantly for the last three days, I think.

ALICE. Me too.

OLIVIA. It's just so lovely to have you home, darling.

ALICE. It's lovely to be home.

OLIVIA. Make sure you come back soon.

ALICE. Come back soon? I'm still here; we haven't even left yet.

OLIVIA. You know what I mean.

ALICE. Yes. I know what you mean.

Beat.

Giles told me you tried to sell the piano.

OLIVIA. Did he?

ALICE. He said you were going to sell it – to just get rid of it.

OLIVIA. We thought about it, yes.

ALICE. Why?

OLIVIA. Why did we want to get rid of it?

ALICE. Yes.

OLIVIA. Because no one ever played it any more. And because your father always thought of you whenever he saw it.

ALICE. So… so why didn't you sell it?

OLIVIA. We had it all ready to go – and as soon as they had moved it out of the drawing room your father told them to stop and put it straight back. And that was that. He said that he wanted to keep it, apologised for wasting their time and gave them some money for their trouble.

ALICE. Why did he change his mind?

OLIVIA. Because the piano isn't his.

ALICE. What?

OLIVIA. Well, I mean, I know it's his; it belongs to your father, and before that it belonged to your father's mother. But to him that piano is yours. He said that when you were little he made up his mind that eventually that piano would be given to you. So selling the piano would have been giving up on the belief that you might come back one day and play it again. And he wasn't prepared to do that. And here you are.

Blackout.

Scene Five

Easter Sunday, 30th March 1997. Evening.

WILLIAM *is sat behind the desk in his study. He has a fountain pen and a book that is open in front of him. The room is clinical – like a headmaster's office. Bookshelves cover most of the wall-space, and are filled with an array of leather-bound books.* GILES *stands by the bookcase.*

GILES. This room. It's… it's pretty much exactly as I remember.

WILLIAM. On the surface maybe, Giles.

GILES. It must be over thirty years since I was last in here.

WILLIAM. If you say so.

GILES. Well, you never invite anyone in here. Least of all me.

WILLIAM. True.

GILES. How many of these books have you read?

WILLIAM. Enough of them to fill a lifetime.

GILES. Roughly. What… half of them?

WILLIAM. Books are odd things. One cannot read all of them; one can only read a number. Having a bookshelf exclusively full of books that you have read is like possessing some kind of literary trophy cabinet; I do not go in for such things.

GILES *pulls a book from one of the shelves.*

GILES. Proust. I've always wanted to read Proust but I've just never got round to it.

WILLIAM. Perhaps one day you will.

GILES. I hope / so.

WILLIAM. Or perhaps you won't. It really doesn't matter. You can either see an unread book as an object that taunts your laziness and ignorance, or an opportunity sitting in front of you just waiting for the time to be right for plucking.

Beat.

GILES. Samuel has probably read most of these, you know…

WILLIAM. I thought he only reads books about space.

GILES. No. He reads everything. He just prefers books about space.

WILLIAM. It's not really reading, though, is it? The way that he reads. He might remember certain passages word for word or whatever it is that he is able to do, but he doesn't really understand the content.

GILES. Ask him. Ask him about some of the books he's read. He'd probably really enjoy that.

WILLIAM. I'm sure he would.

GILES *opens the book and smells the pages.*

I think it's probably about time that you put that book back where you found it and come and sit down.

GILES *replaces the book where he found it, and then sits on the opposite side of the desk to* WILLIAM.

Without going into too much detail, I want to ask you if there is anything in particular of mine that you would like me to leave you in my will.

GILES. Umm…

WILLIAM. I can't make it any clearer.

GILES. Uh…

WILLIAM. Don't umm and ah, Giles. I'm asking you to be decisive. If there is something that you want then you should make it known now.

GILES. Right.

Beat.

WILLIAM. If there is nothing that springs to mind immediately then the answer is no.

GILES. There is something. But I don't know if Alice or Samuel might also –

WILLIAM. I'm not asking them, I'm asking you.

GILES. Yes, but I wouldn't want them –

WILLIAM. This isn't about them, Giles. Just… just tell me what it is.

Beat.

GILES. The painting. In the hallway. Of the two boys playing in the woods.

WILLIAM. I see.

GILES. I've always loved that painting. From when I was young. I don't… I don't even really know why. I just have.

WILLIAM. You have very good taste.

GILES. Well… I don't know about that. I've just always liked it for some reason.

WILLIAM. Oh, I don't doubt that, Giles. I don't doubt that for one moment.

GILES. Right…

WILLIAM. What I do doubt is whether you know the value of that particular painting.

GILES. Its value?

WILLIAM. Yes.

GILES. As in monetary value?

WILLIAM. I would hardly expect you to be able to accurately appraise its artistic value.

GILES. Well, I don't care about its monetary value or its artistic value.

WILLIAM. So you don't know its monetary value?

GILES. No. I don't. I don't know its *monetary* value. And I don't really care to be honest.

WILLIAM. You should care, Giles. You should care a great deal.

GILES. It's not important to me; I don't mind if it's worth everything or nothing at all. But I'd never sell it anyway so it doesn't really matter to me how much it is worth.

Beat.

WILLIAM. Do you think I should leave you the painting?

GILES. I don't… That's up to you.

WILLIAM. You really are a strange boy, Giles.

GILES. Please don't call me a 'boy'. Please don't patronise me / like that.

WILLIAM. Telling me that it's up to me… I am fully aware that it is up to me. That is not the issue. I asked you whether I should leave the painting to you and you shirk the responsibility of answering. You habitually leave the difficult decisions up to other people, and that is the behaviour of a boy. I want to know whether or not you have it in you to stand up and be a man.

GILES. Fine. You want me to stand up then I'll stand up. Yes. You should leave me the painting. Because it means something to me. It reminds me of Samuel and I when we were young. I've always felt that. And it's unique to the painting; I don't get that same feeling – that same memory – from anything else. So yes, you should leave me the painting.

WILLIAM *writes something in his book.*

WILLIAM. The painting is yours.

GILES. Thank you.

WILLIAM. That wasn't so hard, was it?

Beat.

GILES. Is that all?

WILLIAM.…

GILES. Can I go now?

WILLIAM....

> GILES *stands, and walks towards the door.*

> WILLIAM *watches him stride away.*

> (*Suddenly.*) I had an affair.

> *Beat.*

GILES. What did you say?

WILLIAM. Many years ago – when you were a small boy – I had an affair. With a woman. It went on for several years. I've never told anyone.

GILES....

WILLIAM. Your mother doesn't know – to my knowledge. If I am to die before her – or if my memory abandons me altogether – then some trace of this affair may come out. We wrote letters to one another – this woman and I – via Post Office boxes. I kept them. And there are other things – other 'tokens' all here in this room. I can't bring myself to get rid of them. I've tried – on many occasions – but I can't seem to do it.

GILES....

WILLIAM. I know you won't understand. I'm not asking you to. I'm ashamed that it happened – of so many things. She... fell pregnant and I... made it clear that I wanted her to have an abortion. That it was the only way. She was only a young girl. And then after that I just... I deserted her. I had to... there was no other... I just pretended it had never happened. The whole affair broke her in half. She died the following year. 1959. Such a long time ago. I can't really explain.

GILES....

WILLIAM. I know it won't make any difference but... when it became clear to the doctors that your brother wasn't... that he wasn't 'normal' – that's what they said – I took it very badly. I was angry – with myself, with your mother, with the world. With him. And she was... this girl... she was...

GILES. I don't want to know any more.

Short pause.

WILLIAM. Promise me that your mother will never find out about this. Once I'm gone. I need you to… I need you to come in here – on your own – and take care of it. Please, Giles. I need you to do this for me.

GILES.…

WILLIAM. Giles?

WILLIAM *looks at* GILES. *The sense of despair in the room is palpable.* GILES *bows his head to the floor – he cannot bear to look at his father.* GILES *turns and exits.*

WILLIAM *sits at the desk. Seconds pass.*

Blackout.

Scene Six

Easter Sunday, 30th March 1997. Late evening (or more accurately early morning on Easter Monday).

EMILY *and* AURELIA *have snuck out late and raided the booze cabinet. They sit in the kitchen in low light; a selection of liqueur bottles stand on the table.*

EMILY *sips her shot of liqueur.*

AURELIA. Good?

EMILY. That. Is. Vile.

AURELIA. I think just down it.

EMILY. Okay.

EMILY *downs the rest of the shot.*

AURELIA. Better?

EMILY. Not really.

AURELIA. Want to go back to the Baileys?

EMILY. I don't understand why anyone would choose to drink something like that when Baileys is available. I just don't get it.

AURELIA. I'm going to stick with it, I think.

EMILY *pours out another glass of Baileys.*

EMILY. I kind of thought you'd have more of a French accent.

AURELIA. Really?

EMILY. Yeah. I thought you'd be like all 'Nicole? Papa?'…

AURELIA. Who's Nicole?

EMILY. From the advert.

AURELIA. What advert?

EMILY. You know. The car one. 'Nicole? Papa?'…

AURELIA. I don't know what that is.

EMILY. Oh right. Yeah. You probably haven't seen it. Forget it. So… how French are you?

AURELIA. What?

EMILY. Do you… are you, like, properly French? You know, do you think of yourself as French or…? Like when you are just daydreaming and stuff, is it in French or is it in English?

AURELIA. I'm half-English and half-Cameroonian.

EMILY. So… not French at all?

AURELIA. No. Not like in terms of… like… heritage. My mum's English and my dad's from Cameroon. I mean I've pretty much lived in France all my life – so I kind of think of myself as French – like I think I have mostly French sensibilities and everything so… I don't know.

EMILY *pours herself more Baileys.*

EMILY. Should we top up the bottles with water or something?

AURELIA. Really?

EMILY. Well we don't want them to notice, do we?

AURELIA. Who?

EMILY. William.

AURELIA. I know this is probably the wrong thing to say but is he really going to notice? I mean, everyone is saying that… you know… he's starting to forget stuff so, I mean, isn't it quite likely that he won't know how much booze he had in his drinks cabinet?

EMILY. I suppose so; but it wouldn't surprise me if he measured all of his booze… you know… just to try and catch people out.

AURELIA. How can you say that about him? He's your grandfather.

EMILY. So?

AURELIA. So, aren't you supposed to be nice about him?

EMILY. Listen, I don't know what you know about William but he's not the easiest person to be nice about. When William asked me what A levels I was going to study he said 'I doubt anyone has ever got into Oxford University by doing Theatre Studies A level' or something totally undermining like that, and… I mean… it's like not everyone is interested in going to fucking Oxford University, you know? But that's all he bloody cares about or something.

AURELIA. Why do you think he's like that?

EMILY. I guess it's how he was brought up. I think that's always been, like, 'The Pennington Way'. And maybe it's partly something to do with the war as well. I don't know.

AURELIA. Isn't he like a judge or something?

EMILY. Yeah. And he's in the House of Lords, isn't he? He's a Lord of Appeal. An Ordinary one. Or something. Or a Law

Lord. It's really complicated. I don't really get it. But he's just retired, I think – or he's about to. One of the two.

Beat.

AURELIA. My mum never really talks about him.

EMILY. Why not?

AURELIA. I don't know. If ever I used to ask her about him she would say that I'll meet him one day, and then I'd find out for myself.

EMILY. And what do you think now you've met him?

AURELIA. I don't know. I haven't really spent that much time with him yet.

EMILY. And Olivia?

AURELIA. Well, Mum has always brought me over from France pretty much once a year to spend a day with Granny so I know her quite well.

EMILY. Granny? Do you call her Granny?

AURELIA. Yeah.

EMILY. What about William? Do you call him Granddad?

AURELIA. I only met him for the first time on Friday.

EMILY. What, so he couldn't be bothered to come over with Olivia to see you?

AURELIA. My mum and Granny kept the whole thing a secret actually – from William and everyone – but Mum told everyone else about it yesterday. Apparently. So the secret's out now.

EMILY. No one told me.

AURELIA. Well, you know now.

Pause. AURELIA *downs her shot.*

EMILY. That's the problem with this family; there's always something going on that someone hasn't told you about. And then you find out years after the event. It's so fucked up.

AURELIA. I think that's normal.

Beat.

EMILY. Aren't you mad? Like angry mad.

AURELIA. About what?

Suddenly WILLIAM *appears at the door.*

WILLIAM. What's going on?

EMILY *and* AURELIA *are both startled;* EMILY *lets out a guilty shriek and then tries to conceal the alcohol, while* AURELIA *looks on.*

EMILY. Ugh! You startled me.

WILLIAM. What time is it?

EMILY. I don't know.

WILLIAM *looks at the clock on the wall.*

WILLIAM. It's nearly two in the morning.

EMILY. Is it? We didn't realise.

WILLIAM. What are you girls even doing in here?

EMILY. Nothing. Just talking really.

AURELIA. And we decided to have a drink.

EMILY *shoots a 'What are you doing?' look at* AURELIA.

WILLIAM. What did you say, girl?

AURELIA. I said we decided to have a drink. Or two. I hope that's all right. We couldn't sleep.

WILLIAM. Me neither. I can't seem to escape the day.

Beat.

EMILY (*to* AURELIA). Maybe we should…

WILLIAM. What are you drinking?

AURELIA. White sambuca.

WILLIAM. How would you like to have a glass of a Benromach Single Malt that is older than the both of you put together? It is my birthday today after all.

EMILY. I… it's late. I think I should probably go to bed now.

WILLIAM. Yes. Perhaps you should. (*To* AURELIA.) And you? Want to run away to bed like your cousin?

AURELIA *looks at* EMILY*; she is torn.*

AURELIA. I'll join you for a drink.

WILLIAM. That's the spirit.

WILLIAM *heads to the drinks cabinet, while* EMILY *makes her way to the door.*

EMILY. Happy birthday, William.

WILLIAM (*turning to look at* EMILY). Sleep well.

AURELIA. Goodnight, Emily.

EMILY *glowers at* AURELIA*, then exits.*

WILLIAM *has the bottle of whisky, and two whisky glasses, in hand – and makes his way to the table.*

WILLIAM *sets the glasses down and pours a healthy amount of whisky into each glass.*

WILLIAM. We're going to drink this neat. I'm afraid I have to insist.

AURELIA. Okay.

WILLIAM *passes* AURELIA *her glass – then raises his own.*

WILLIAM. Cheers.

AURELIA. Cheers.

They clink their glasses – then both take a sip. WILLIAM *half-expects* AURELIA *to splutter, but she doesn't.*

WILLIAM. I am very pleased to have you here, you know.

AURELIA....

WILLIAM. And I want you to know that I have thought of you.

AURELIA. Sorry?

WILLIAM. Just in case you didn't think I did. Every year, on your birthday, I would make sure to think of you. Even just for a short moment. April 20th. On the cusp, you see. On the cusp of being an Aries like me, and a Taurus like Olivia. Not that I believe in any of that nonsense. But every year. April 20th. I'd think about you; in my own way.

AURELIA....

WILLIAM. Could you... would you tell me some of the things you like?

AURELIA. Like what?

WILLIAM. Or that you don't like. Anything.

WILLIAM *takes a larger sip of whisky.*

Beat.

AURELIA. I... I like... I like music. Umm... I like animals...

WILLIAM. Most people like music and animals. Saying that doesn't tell me anything about you. I want details. If you can give them to me. Specific to you.

AURELIA *takes a sip of whisky.*

AURELIA. I like cold showers on hot days, and hot showers on cold days.

WILLIAM. That's also fairly common.

AURELIA. I don't like novels unless they are written in the first person.

WILLIAM. Why not?

AURELIA. I just don't.

WILLIAM. Okay.

AURELIA. I… only like bananas that have at least a bit of brown on the skin somewhere. I… like swimming underwater but I don't really like swimming on the surface. I… like going to bed knowing that I did one thing in the day that I hadn't ever done before. I… like making lists up on the spot.

WILLIAM. Try not to think too hard. Keep going.

AURELIA. I like being outside. Alone. Maybe in a field. Or on a hillside. Completely alone. So that in that moment it's possible that I'm the only person alive. And then I like seeing someone else appear in the distance so I know that I'm not. I think that's… I hope that's specific enough for you.

AURELIA takes a large gulp of whisky.

WILLIAM. Thank you for that.

AURELIA.…

WILLIAM. It's not a… I'm playing catch-up a little bit with Olivia when it comes to finding out all about you, so thank you for indulging me.

AURELIA. No, it's…

WILLIAM. I'd try and guess sometimes what sort of things you would like. If I were to get you a present, what sort of thing you would like, and what you wouldn't. A book of some description. A toy. A dress. What would you have liked? It used to… it used to play on my mind from time to time.

Beat.

AURELIA. I call her Granny, you know.

WILLIAM. What?

AURELIA. She lets me. She never… she never said I shouldn't.

WILLIAM.…

AURELIA. And I'd like to call you Granddad.

WILLIAM. I… no, I'd rather you didn't.

AURELIA. You just asked me about the things that I'd like. And I'd like to call you Granddad.

WILLIAM. That's… that's not the same as…

AURELIA. You'd prefer it if I just called you William?

WILLIAM. That's the… that's the drill, yes.

AURELIA. But I already know people called William. There was a boy at my school called William. Guillaume. And there are hundreds of people. Thousands. Tens of thousands. Millions maybe. All called William. Anyone can be a William. But you're… I don't have another Granddad. My father's father died before I was born. I only have you. And maybe that's… I don't know. If I can't call you Granddad then that's… Especially now. After waiting so long to… it would be a real shame I think, not to… Don't you?

Blackout.

ACT FIVE

Scene One

Easter Monday, 31st March 1997. Morning. WILLIAM*'s birthday.*

The drawing room.

EMILY *is sitting on an armchair; she is reading a glossy magazine.* ALICE *is sitting on another armchair – and is writing a card.*

EMILY *turns the page – but is more interested in* ALICE.

EMILY. What are you writing?

ALICE....

EMILY. Never mind.

ALICE. Sorry?

EMILY. Oh... I was just wondering what you were writing.

ALICE. William's birthday card.

EMILY. Really? You've been doing it for ages.

ALICE. I know.

EMILY. I just write 'Happy Birthday' and then like maybe a kiss or a few kisses. And my name. Obviously.

ALICE. Obviously.

EMILY. Where's Aurelia?

ALICE. She's having a bit of a lie-in; I think the weekend might have caught up with her a bit.

EMILY. Well, she was up quite late.

ALICE. Up late?

EMILY. Yeah. We were in the kitchen last night having a bit of a chat and stuff – and then William came down and joined us.

ALICE. He… what…?

EMILY. He came and sat with us. Opened some special bottle of whisky and wanted to have a birthday drink with us. I mean, I thought it was probably some kind of trick or something, so I went to bed straight away – I really hate whisky – but I guess they must have probably stayed up for a bit.

Beat.

Can I ask you something?

ALICE. What?

EMILY. I was thinking about it last night and… well… what made you come back?

ALICE. Sorry?

EMILY. After so long. After staying away so long. What made you come now?

Beat.

ALICE. Aurelia.

EMILY.…

ALICE. I told her that we'd been invited over for William's birthday – that we'd both been invited – and she said that we should come.

EMILY. And that was it?

ALICE. I think she thought that enough time had passed for everyone to just get on with things as they are.

EMILY. Was she right?

ALICE.…

Beat.

EMILY. It's hard, though, isn't it?

ALICE....

EMILY. It's like... well, when things happen it's so hard to just forget it all, isn't it? Like you want everything to be fine, but sometimes it just isn't, and before you know it people are saying things, and doing things, and maybe throwing things, and you really just want to turn around and face the other way and pretend that none of that even exists. Don't you?

ALICE. Something like that...

EMILY. Like there's this girl at my school that I fell out with when we were in the upper fourth and that's it as far as I'm concerned. Doesn't matter whether she apologises to me or not, I know what she's like – a complete bitch – and she's nailed her colours to the mast and so that's it. Done and dusted. Her loss.

ALICE *looks down at what she has written in the card.*

ALICE. Do you think you did anything wrong though?

EMILY. What – to Caroline Longstaff?

ALICE. Like did you behave in a way that was – I don't know – confrontational, or angry, or spiteful, or...?

EMILY. Yeah, you bet I did. Why should I just roll over and let her spread lies about me?

ALICE. Then maybe it's difficult for her as well.

EMILY. So? I don't care about her. I hope it is difficult for her. I hope she hates herself.

EMILY *jumps to her feet.*

I think I should probably go and wake up Sleeping Beauty.

And EMILY *is gone before* ALICE *can even respond.*

ALICE *finishes writing the card. She blows on the ink and puts the card into the envelope, then seals it. She gets to her feet, places the card on the mantelpiece, and then makes her way to the hallway – but is stopped by the arrival of* WILLIAM; *who is wearing a smart blazer and tie.*

ALICE. Happy birthday!

WILLIAM. Yes.

There is a moment where an embrace might occur, but the instinct is swallowed by both of them.

ALICE. How are you feeling?

WILLIAM. Old. Feeble.

ALICE. Are you fishing for a compliment?

WILLIAM. Hardly. Although I wouldn't turn one away if it knocked at my door.

Beat.

ALICE. Did you sleep well?

WILLIAM. Not at first. Second time was a charm though.

ALICE. Emily said you were up quite late.

WILLIAM. Later than normal, yes.

Beat.

ALICE. I've written you a card. It's over there on the mantelpiece.

WILLIAM. Right. Well, thank you.

ALICE. Please don't let anyone else see it.

WILLIAM. Think they'll all want one, do you?

ALICE. I'm serious. I don't want anyone else to read it.

WILLIAM. No, of course.

ALICE. And I don't want to talk about it. I've written what I wanted to say. And as far as I'm concerned, that's it.

WILLIAM. I understand.

ALICE *and* WILLIAM *stand in front of one another for a long moment.*

ALICE. I should probably go and check on Aurelia. Make sure she hasn't got too much of a headache.

WILLIAM. Good idea.

WILLIAM *walks into the drawing room, making space for* ALICE *to head past him out towards the hallway.*

ALICE. Happy birthday.

And ALICE *is gone. Leaving* WILLIAM *alone. He walks slowly, and with some reservation, towards the mantelpiece. He picks up the envelope, opens it, and removes the card. He takes his reading glasses out of his pocket and puts them on.*

WILLIAM *reads the card. He struggles with his emotions, but manages to get through it. He then places the card back in its envelope and puts it in his blazer pocket, and takes his glasses off.*

Blackout.

Scene Two

Easter Monday, 31st March 1997. Early afternoon.

The drawing room.

SOPHIE *is sitting on an armchair –* EMILY *on the settee; they hold a wrapped present each.*

EMILY. How long is this going to take?

SOPHIE. Not long.

EMILY. Well, how long is that?

SOPHIE. I don't know.

Beat.

EMILY (*holding up the present*). What is this?

SOPHIE. It's a book about cricket.

EMILY. Brilliant. A book. About cricket. How original.

SOPHIE. William doesn't want anything original. He wants things he's asked for. And he asked for the cricket book.

EMILY. Still…

SOPHIE. Still what? When you want to take the time and effort to go shopping for people's presents then you can get whatever you like. But when you leave it to me then you should really have the decency not to moan about it.

Beat.

EMILY. Are you all right, Mum?

SOPHIE. I'm fine, I just… it's a long weekend and I'm tired and… I'm fine. I'm fine.

EMILY. Is everyone else coming or…?

SOPHIE. They'll be here soon.

EMILY. Soon like five minutes?

SOPHIE. Oh, I don't know, Emily.

EMILY. It's not an unreasonable thing to ask, you know, Mum; I only want to know what's going on. It's nice to be told what's going on every now and then. Rather than just being told to 'sit down and wait'.

SOPHIE. Well, 'sit down and wait' is all I know so far.

AURELIA *appears at the door; she also carries a wrapped present.*

AURELIA. We're about to do presents, is that right?

EMILY. Apparently.

SOPHIE (*to* AURELIA). Yes, that's right.

AURELIA *walks tentatively over to a settee and sits down.*

EMILY (*looking at* AURELIA*'s present*). Looks like a big book.

AURELIA. Sort of. I hope he likes it. I didn't really know what to get him.

SOPHIE. Didn't your mum help you choose it?

AURELIA. Umm… I didn't choose it, I made it.

EMILY. Cool. I used to make presents for people. When I was like six.

There is an uncomfortable pause. AURELIA *tries to change the conversation.*

AURELIA. Umm… you know the portrait – the painting at the top of the stairs; who is that?

SOPHIE. That's your great-great-grandfather. William's grandfather.

AURELIA. He looks a lot like Uncle Samuel.

SOPHIE. Yes. I suppose he does.

SIMON *enters – also carrying a wrapped present. He walks purposefully to a chair and sits down.*

EMILY. What did you get him?

No response from SIMON *– he either does not hear her or deliberately ignores her.*

Er… hello! Simon! What have you got for William?

SIMON. Just wait and see.

EMILY. What? Just tell me.

SIMON. No.

EMILY (*to* SOPHIE). Do you know what Simon got?

SOPHIE. No. He bought it himself.

SIMON. Do you even know what *you've* got?

EMILY. Yes. Actually. I do.

SIMON. What is it then?

EMILY. A book. About cricket.

SIMON. What's it called?

EMILY. I don't know what it's *called*, Simon. But I know what it *is*.

GILES *enters, closely followed by* SAMUEL – *who is carrying two wrapped presents.*

AURELIA. Ooh! That's a big present, Uncle Samuel. Can I see?

SAMUEL. Yes.

SAMUEL *sits down on the settee with* AURELIA. *The atmosphere in the room is slightly strained.* GILES *and* SOPHIE *can barely look at one another.*

AURELIA. It's very well wrapped.

SAMUEL. Yes. Giles did help me though. He measured the paper, and then cut it out for me. Didn't you, Giles?

GILES *is no longer listening.* ALICE *enters – she also holds a wrapped present.*

Giles! Didn't you?

GILES. Didn't I what?

SAMUEL. Help me.

GILES. Yes.

SAMUEL. With the wrapping.

GILES. Yes.

ALICE. You sound pretty excited, Samuel.

SAMUEL. If the excitement scale runs from one to ten I would say that I am a seven point nine.

ALICE. That's very precise.

SAMUEL. Yes.

Beat.

ALICE. You used to love it when it was your birthday. Do you still love it?

SAMUEL. Yes and no.

ALICE. Yes because…

SAMUEL. Yes because Olivia makes me a special cake and I get presents.

OLIVIA and WILLIAM *enter the room; nobody notices.*

ALICE. Right. And no because…

SAMUEL. No because I can feel quite lonely because I do not have very many friends. I always wanted to have a big party with lots of friends – like in the film *Parenthood* with Steve Martin where he's Cowboy Gil and they have all games and everything – but I can't really because it would just be me and Olivia and Giles like normal.

Beat.

OLIVIA. Oh. We're all here. Very well done, everyone.

There are half-hearted cheers and general birthday greetings from everyone as they see WILLIAM *for the first time.*

WILLIAM. Yes, well, let's not make a big song and dance.

WILLIAM *and* OLIVIA *move towards their 'designated seats' in the room.*

OLIVIA. Oh. You make it sound like we've planned some kind of grand ceremony.

WILLIAM. No fuss.

OLIVIA. Okay. No fuss. We'll just do presents and that's it. So who wants to go first?

Nobody moves. WILLIAM *is now sat down.*

EMILY. I'll go first.

EMILY *rises and takes her present over to* WILLIAM. *He holds it in his hand.*

WILLIAM. It's a book, isn't it?

EMILY. Oh, just open it.

OLIVIA. It's lovely wrapping paper. Where did you get it from?

WILLIAM. That's all I need. *Another* book.

EMILY. Mum got the wrapping paper.

OLIVIA. Where did you get the paper, Sophie?

SOPHIE. Oh. Nowhere special.

> WILLIAM *opens the present. The others gently coo and make noises that convey a mild level of (mostly feigned) curiosity. He looks at the book.*

EMILY. I remember you mentioning that you wanted it. I can't remember exactly but…

WILLIAM. Yes. Thank you.

SIMON (*to* EMILY). What's it called?

WILLIAM. *Rain Men: The Madness of Cricket.* By Marcus Berkmann. Just in time for the season.

SOPHIE. That is the one you wanted, isn't it, William?

WILLIAM. Yes.

SOPHIE. Good.

WILLIAM. Well, I very much look forward to reading that over the course of the summer; it should help distract me from another year of Ashes disappointment.

> WILLIAM *puts the book down.* GILES *rises and walks towards the door.*

OLIVIA. Giles?

> GILES *turns back.*

GILES. Yes?

OLIVIA. Where are you going?

GILES. To get a drink.

OLIVIA. Do you have to get one right now?

GILES. Yes, I do actually.

GILES *exits*.

OLIVIA (*to* SOPHIE). Is he all right? He's been very quiet all day.

SOPHIE. He hasn't said anything to me, so…

WILLIAM. Come on. Let's get this over and done with as soon as we can.

AURELIA. You're supposed to enjoy the suspense. You're supposed to want to draw it out.

ALICE. I think the birthday boy protests too much; I think he loves having all the attention.

WILLIAM. Well, I hate to be the one to break it to you but he really doesn't.

ALICE (*playfully*). Oh, just shut up and open your presents.

WILLIAM. Yes, yes.

ALICE. And try to at least *act* grateful.

OLIVIA. Samuel? Do you want to give William your present?

SAMUEL *picks up his present and takes it over to* WILLIAM.

SAMUEL. I saw it in the shop and I liked it straight away.

WILLIAM *opens the present*. SAMUEL *stands beside him. It is something in a medium-sized frame*. GILES *enters with a glass in his hand, and looks on from the doorway.*

WILLIAM. What on earth is this?

SAMUEL. It's a 'magic eye' picture.

WILLIAM. A magic what?

SAMUEL. It shouldn't really be called magic because really it's just physics – which is the opposite of magic – so that's a bit odd. It's really called an autostereogram, and if you look at it the right way then you can see a three dimensional image

within the two dimensions of the picture. I won't tell you
what the 3D image is, because I saw it before I bought it, but
it's really good fun trying to see it. And it's a very interesting
colourful picture anyway. I got it framed so you can put it on
the wall and then you can look at it whenever you want.
That's what I would do anyway.

OLIVIA. Well, what a lovely present, Samuel.

SAMUEL. Yes. Giles took me shopping especially and when I
saw it I thought 'That's the ticket.'

Beat.

WILLIAM. I am completely bemused by this.

OLIVIA. Just say thank you, William.

WILLIAM. I suppose it's the thought that counts. Even if the
thought is completely ludicrous.

SIMON. Well, I think it's actually a rather brilliant present,
Uncle Samuel.

SAMUEL. Yes. I think so.

WILLIAM. Excuse me but at what point have I ever shown an
interest in novelties and gimmicks?

OLIVIA. Oh, please.

GILES. Open my present.

GILES *walks over from the doorway – picks up the present
he had left where he had previously been sitting – and
carries it over to* WILLIAM, *who has difficulty unwrapping
the present.*

WILLIAM. You've wrapped it so tight I can't...

OLIVIA. Let me see.

WILLIAM. No, no. It's fine.

WILLIAM *is still struggling.*

OLIVIA. Do you want a knife?

WILLIAM. No. I'll just… you've used so much blasted tape…

ALICE. Come on, just –

WILLIAM. I don't need any help.

ALICE. There's no hurry.

WILLIAM. The paper's too taut.

SIMON. Let's do a countdown. Ten. Nine.

SIMON/SAMUEL. Eight.

ALICE. Stop milking it.

SIMON/SAMUEL/
    AURELIA. Seven. Six.

SIMON/SAMUEL/
    AURELIA. Five. Four.

WILLIAM. I can't get any purchase.

I'm not!

SIMON. Come on! Just rip it!

You're running out of time.

SIMON/SAMUEL/AURELIA/EMILY. Three. Two. One.

    SIMON *makes an alarm sound.*

SAMUEL. Lift-off!

OLIVIA. I'll get the scissors.

    OLIVIA *rises and exits.*

WILLIAM. What the hell is wrong with you, Giles? I mean, who wraps a present like that? What the hell is in here? Weapons-grade plutonium?

SAMUEL. Giles. Lift-off!

GILES. I just wrapped it normally.

WILLIAM. Well, it seems that / what is normal for you, Giles…

SAMUEL. Giles? Lift-off! Like when we went in the shuttle.

WILLIAM. …isn't exactly normal for the rest of us.

SAMUEL. Giles? Do you remember that? Doing the countdown.

WILLIAM. Oh, do stop squawking, Samuel.

SAMUEL. Giles? In Cape Canaveral? Do you remember?

WILLIAM. What? What are you talking about now?

SAMUEL. When Giles and I went in a space shuttle.

WILLIAM. What?

SAMUEL. In Cape Canaveral.

WILLIAM. What are you… you did no such thing. Now be quiet!

OLIVIA *re-enters, scissors in hand.*

SAMUEL. Yes we did. We went into space.

WILLIAM (*starting to get incensed*). Into space? To Cape Canaveral? What the hell are you talking about? All these idiotic little stories.

GILES. Don't talk to him like that.

WILLIAM. You've never been anywhere in your entire life!

GILES. Yes he has!

WILLIAM. Have you gone –

GILES. He *has* been there. He *has* been to Cape Canaveral. And he *has* been in a space shuttle.

WILLIAM. Has everyone suddenly gone mad?

GILES. We play it like it's really happening. And it's not *real*. But to him it *feels* real.

WILLIAM. What the hell are you talking about, Giles?

GILES. We pretend. We watch something; then we act it out.

WILLIAM. What, when you were children? Is that what you're talking about? When you were children?

GILES. That's when it started.

WILLIAM. And when did it stop?

GILES. It hasn't stopped. We still do it. We play adventures. Once a week. Just like we always have.

WILLIAM. Don't you think that's rather pathetic for a grown man?

GILES. I'm a grown man now, am I? You're done with calling me 'boy' and 'child'?

WILLIAM. You're a doctor, for Christ's sake, Giles!

GILES. I knew you wouldn't understand. It's just… it's beyond you.

GILES *walks to the doorway – where he stands for a second as if to say something.*

I need… I can't stand this. Being here and… with everything that's… I need to get away, I…

GILES *exits.*

SIMON. What just happened?

WILLIAM. I think they call it a mid-life crisis.

OLIVIA. Oh, shut up, William! Just shut up! Shut up! Shut up!

OLIVIA *storms out the room.*

ALICE *takes a moment before following after* OLIVIA – *looking at* WILLIAM *with resigned derision as she goes.*

SOPHIE. Do you know what? I have something that I want to say. And it's something I've been meaning to say for a long time. Giles tries… so hard… And you, William… you just refuse to see it. And I really don't understand why.

SIMON *stands – takes his present over to where* WILLIAM *is and puts it next to him – and then walks out the room.*

By now WILLIAM *has opened the present from* GILES.

They're Romeo and Julietas. They're the ones Churchill smoked apparently.

WILLIAM.…

WILLIAM *opens the box and smells the cigars.*

EMILY (*under her breath*). Mum…

SOPHIE *nods – and she and* EMILY *quickly leave the room.*

WILLIAM (*to* AURELIA). Don't you want to scarper off as well?

AURELIA. Yes. I do.

WILLIAM. Well, go on then.

AURELIA. No. I'm going to stay.

WILLIAM. And why's that then?

AURELIA. Someone has to.

SAMUEL *and* AURELIA *sit in silence as* WILLIAM *opens his presents.*

Blackout.

Scene Three

Easter Monday, 31st March 1997. Late afternoon.

Drawing room. WILLIAM *is asleep in his chair – he is wearing a new jumper – a birthday gift.* OLIVIA *is cleaning up the room; she starts gathering the discarded wrapping paper from the floor, putting it into a plastic bag.*

AURELIA *enters.*

AURELIA. Do you want me to do that, Granny?

OLIVIA. Would you mind?

AURELIA. No, not at all.

OLIVIA *hands* AURELIA *the bag.*

OLIVIA. Thank you.

AURELIA. It's no bother.

OLIVIA. It's been a long weekend.

AURELIA. Yes.

> OLIVIA *sits down in her chair.*

OLIVIA. Easter is supposed to be a four-day holiday; it never quite works out that way, though, does it?

> AURELIA *sees* WILLIAM *sleep in the chair.*

AURELIA (*whispering – pointing at* WILLIAM). Oh. I didn't see him there.

OLIVIA. Oh, don't worry about him. He's fast asleep.

AURELIA. Are you sure?

> OLIVIA *looks at* AURELIA *as if to say – 'This is my specialist subject.'*

> SIMON *enters. He is carrying a box of old books; it is the same box seen earlier in Scene One.*

SIMON. Is Dad back yet?

OLIVIA. His car wasn't in the driveway last time I checked. Why?

SIMON. Uncle Samuel and I just found this box of some of his old exercise books from school in the barn. I thought he might want to look through them.

OLIVIA. Well, can you put them in the kitchen in the meantime?

SIMON. Sure.

> SIMON *exits.*

OLIVIA. He said some rather lovely things about you this morning.

AURELIA. Really?

OLIVIA. A lot like your mother. Is what he said.

AURELIA. Right.

Suddenly WILLIAM *emits a strong nasal snore.* AURELIA
*jumps slightly from the shock of it. The snoring continues; it
is a low, solid snore – like a dull murmur.*

OLIVIA. Ah. The snoring. It was just a matter of time really.

AURELIA. Ha!

OLIVIA. Well, now he's started let's leave him to it.

OLIVIA *and* AURELIA *exit towards the kitchen.*

SAMUEL *wanders slowly and carefully into the drawing
room. He looks over at* WILLIAM *and notices that he is fast
asleep. He walks over to the 'magic eye' picture that leans
against the side of William's chair. He picks it up, then walks
over to the settee, and sits down. He lays the 'magic eye'
picture on his lap and stares at it for a short while – until he
sees the 3D image. His face lights up. He then lifts the
picture off his lap, stands up, and returns it to the side of
William's chair. But the picture is not balanced properly, and
it falls flat onto the ground, making a clattering noise that
wakes* WILLIAM *with a start – he looks at* SAMUEL *and
mistakes him for his own grandfather;* WILLIAM *believes
he is back in 1942.*

WILLIAM. Grandfather?

SAMUEL. Oh no. Sorry. I was trying so hard to be quiet.

WILLIAM. Is there any word?

SAMUEL. What word? What does that mean?

SAMUEL *is thrown completely.*

I don't know what to say.

WILLIAM. Is it bad news?

SAMUEL. I don't have any news at all.

WILLIAM. Thank God; I thought that was why you woke me.

SAMUEL. I didn't mean to wake you up. It was an accident.

WILLIAM. Yes. Sorry. You said.

Beat.

SAMUEL. You sound funny.

WILLIAM. Do I? I'm just… I'm just worried, I guess.

SAMUEL. Worried about what?

WILLIAM. About Nicholas. About what's going on over there. About going back. All manner of things, in truth.

SAMUEL. You shouldn't worry. 'Worry often gives a small thing a big shadow.' That's what Janet says. When I worry about things.

Beat.

WILLIAM. It's cold in here.

SAMUEL. When I'm cold I get a blanket. It always works.

WILLIAM. Yes. A blanket. That's a good idea.

SAMUEL. Yes.

Beat.

WILLIAM. Could you pass me the blanket on the chair?

SAMUEL. Yes.

SAMUEL *walks to the chair and picks up the blanket before taking it over to* WILLIAM.

WILLIAM. Thank you.

SAMUEL. I can tuck you in if you like.

WILLIAM. Okay.

SAMUEL *tucks the blanket around* WILLIAM.

SAMUEL. Do you want to go back to sleep now?

WILLIAM. Yes. Maybe I will.

SAMUEL. Sleep well.

WILLIAM. Right. Yes. Well, thank you for looking in on me.

SAMUEL *exits the drawing room into the hallway.* GILES *enters the hallway from the front door.*

SAMUEL. Where did you go?

GILES. Nowhere in particular.

Beat.

SAMUEL. Who's Nicholas?

GILES. Nicholas? I don't know. Why?

SAMUEL. William was just talking about Nicholas.

GILES. What did he say?

SAMUEL. He said he was worried about Nicholas. And then I tucked him in with a blanket.

Beat.

GILES. Right. Okay.

SAMUEL. I thought that maybe that he meant Uncle Nicholas, but William always said that Uncle Nicholas died in the war, so that would be silly.

GILES. Yes.

SAMUEL. I'm quite thirsty.

GILES....

SAMUEL. I'm quite thirsty.

Beat.

GILES. Okay. Umm... go into the kitchen. I'll make you a drink in a minute.

SAMUEL. I'd like squash.

GILES. Whatever you want, Samuel.

SAMUEL. I want squash.

SAMUEL *walks off to the kitchen.*

GILES *heads into the drawing room. He sees* WILLIAM *asleep in the chair, and approaches slowly. He stands over him for a short while – like a father keeping watch on his sleeping, sickly child.*

Blackout.

Scene Four

The drawing room.

WILLIAM *is still in his chair. Stock still, he stares out blankly in front of him.*

OLIVIA *enters.*

OLIVIA. William?

    WILLIAM *does not register.*

    William!

WILLIAM. Sorry; I was miles away.

OLIVIA. I thought we should probably do the cake now.

WILLIAM. Yes. That's probably a good idea.

OLIVIA. Do you want to do it in the kitchen or in here?

WILLIAM. In here I think.

OLIVIA. Okay.

    WILLIAM *looks at* OLIVIA.

WILLIAM. You look very pretty.

    Beat.

OLIVIA. I don't think you're allowed to call a woman of my age pretty.

WILLIAM. You'll always be a pretty young thing to me.

OLIVIA. Oh, stop it.

WILLIAM. I will not stop it.

OLIVIA. You can say I'm beautiful if you like. But not pretty.

WILLIAM. Very well. You look beautiful.

OLIVIA. Well, thank you.

GILES *enters carrying an old exercise book.*

GILES. Have you seen Samuel?

OLIVIA. I think we're going to do the cake now.

GILES. Where's Samuel though?

OLIVIA. I don't know. But can you tell everyone to come in here so we can do the birthday cake?

GILES. Now?

OLIVIA. Yes now.

GILES *puts the book down on the side table by the door and exits.*

WILLIAM. Those boys are completely inseparable, aren't they?

OLIVIA. Yes.

WILLIAM. It's funny how it comes so naturally to some people and not at all to others.

OLIVIA. What does?

WILLIAM. Just… being there.

GILES *and* SAMUEL *enter.*

GILES. Look at this.

SAMUEL. At what?

GILES *picks up the exercise book from the side table, and pulls out a loose piece of paper.*

OLIVIA. Did you manage to tell everyone?

GILES. Yes. They're coming.

OLIVIA. Right.

> OLIVIA *exits*. GILES *passes* SAMUEL *the piece of paper.*

GILES. I found it tucked away in one of my old exercise books.

SAMUEL. That's my handwriting.

GILES. Yes. You wrote it down so I could learn it. Do you remember?

> SAMUEL *studies the piece of paper.*

SAMUEL. It's *Doctor Who*.

GILES. I think it must have been one of the first ones. A Hartnell.

SAMUEL. Yes.

GILES. We watched it on the television and then you wrote it down.

SAMUEL. Yes.

GILES. Do you know when that was?

SAMUEL. William Hartnell. 1963 to 1966. Then again in 1972 to '73 for *The Three Doctors*.

GILES. Blimey, that's…

SAMUEL. Quite a long time ago now.

GILES. When we were boys.

WILLIAM. What are you two going on about?

GILES. It's nothing.

SAMUEL. It's *Doctor Who*.

GILES. It's really nothing.

WILLIAM. Then why are you both so excited?

SAMUEL. I haven't played this *Doctor Who* for quite some time.

WILLIAM. What is this? Is this... is this one of your games?

GILES. So what if it is?

SAMUEL. It's very old indeed.

WILLIAM. So how do you play it?

Beat.

GILES. Why do you want to know?

WILLIAM. I'm interested.

GILES. You're interested?

SAMUEL. He's interested, Giles.

GILES. All of a sudden you're interested?

WILLIAM. I didn't know anything about this until earlier today; it would have been hard to be interested before that. So how do you... how do you play?

GILES. We just act it out.

WILLIAM. Show me.

GILES. We're not going to show you.

WILLIAM. What about you, Samuel? Do you want to show me?

GILES. Don't do that.

SAMUEL. Show you?

GILES. Don't try and trick him.

SAMUEL. Show you what?

WILLIAM. Show me the game. Show me *Doctor Who*.

GILES. We're not going to show you.

WILLIAM. I'd genuinely like to see. Is that so hard to believe, Giles?

GILES. Frankly, yes it is.

SAMUEL. Umm… Yes. Show you *Doctor Who*. Yes. Take the paper, and then we can start.

Beat.

GILES. I don't know about this, Samuel. Do you want William to watch? You don't have to say yes, all right? This is our thing, remember. Do we want William to see it?

SAMUEL. Yes. William to see it. Yes.

GILES *looks at* WILLIAM *uncomfortably.*

GILES. Okay. Whatever you want, Samuel.

SAMUEL *hands* GILES *the paper.* SAMUEL *adopts his starting position.* GILES *looks at the paper – he tries to do his best to pretend* WILLIAM *is not in the room.*

'Doctor – some very strange things are happening. I feel we're in a very dangerous position; this is no time for personal quarrels.'

SAMUEL. 'Meaning?'

GILES. 'I think you should go and apologise to Barbara at once.'

SAMUEL. 'I'm afraid we have no time for codes and manners. And I certainly don't underestimate the dangers if they exist. But I must have time to think. I must think. Rash action is worse than no action at all. Hmmm?'

GILES. 'I don't see anything rash in apologising to Barbara. Frankly, Doctor, I find it hard to keep pace with you.'

SAMUEL. 'You mean to keep one jump ahead – that you will never be. You need my knowledge and ability to apply it, and then you need my experience to gain the fullest results.'

GILES. 'Results? For good or for evil?'

SAMUEL. 'One man's law is another man's crime. Sleep on it, Chesterton. Sleep on it.'

GILES *and* SAMUEL *both freeze. Pause. Then suddenly* GILES *breaks.* WILLIAM *has been silent and still throughout.*

GILES. Was that all right?

SAMUEL. Exactly right. Perfect, perfect, perfect. Just like the real *Doctor Who.*

GILES *looks towards* WILLIAM – *who is watching intently.*

GILES. Samuel, why don't you go and see if Olivia wants any help with the cake? She's in the kitchen.

SAMUEL. The cake. Yes.

GILES. You can help her light the candles.

SAMUEL. Light the candles. Yes.

SAMUEL *exits happily.*

GILES. Go on then; you must have something you want to say.

WILLIAM. You want to know what I think?

GILES....

WILLIAM. I think he's lucky to have you as a brother.

Beat.

GILES. What?

WILLIAM. He's very lucky. You're a very wonderful brother to that boy.

GILES *does not know what to say.*

GILES. Is that jumper new?

WILLIAM. A birthday present from your mother.

GILES. It looks good; looks like a perfect fit.

WILLIAM. I guess your mother has sized me up pretty well by now.

Beat.

I can't undo the things I've done, Giles.

GILES. I know.

Suddenly the lights in the room dim and are replaced by flickering candlelight.

SIMON *enters – carrying the cake – followed by* OLIVIA, ALICE, AURELIA, EMILY, SOPHIE *and* SAMUEL.

They all sing 'Happy Birthday' to WILLIAM. *Clapping and laughter.*

SAMUEL. Make a wish!

WILLIAM *blows out the candles.*

Darkness.

End.

Other Titles in this Series

A Nick Hern Book

The Gathered Leaves first published in Great Britain as a paperback original in 2015 by Nick Hern Books Limited, The Glasshouse, 49a Goldhawk Road, London W12 8QP, in association with Dead Letter Perfect and Park Theatre, London

The Gathered Leaves copyright © 2015 Andrew Keatley

Andrew Keatley has asserted his right to be identified as the author of this work

Extract from *Doctor Who: The Edge of Destruction* by David Whitaker reproduced with kind permission by Ken Soutar, PO Box 254, Turramurra, NSW, 2074 Australia, as Trustee for Kyle McIntosh, owner of the rights for the late David Whitaker

Cover image: N9Design.com

Designed and typeset by Nick Hern Books, London
Printed in the UK by CPI Group (UK) Ltd

A CIP catalogue record for this book is available from the British Library

ISBN   978 1 84842 490 6

www.nickhernbooks.co.uk

facebook.com/nickhernbooks

twitter.com/nickhernbooks